I Can, I Will, I Must!

Kevin B DiBacco

Pharos Books

The author has attempted to present information that is as accurate and concrete as possible. The author is not a medical doctor and does not write in any medical capacity. All medical decisions should be made under the guidance and care of your primary physician. The author will not be held liable for any injury or loss that is incurred to the reader through the application of any of the information herein, contained in this book. The author makes it clear that the medical field is fast evolving with newer studies being done continuously, therefore the information in this book is only a researched collaboration of accurate information at the time of writing. With the ever-changing nature of the subjects included, the author hopes that the reader will be able to appreciate the content that has been covered in this book. While all attempts have been made to verify each piece of information provided in this publication, the author assumes no responsibility for any error, omission, or contrary interpretation of the subject matter present in this book. Please note that any help or advice given hereof is not a substitution for licensed medical advice. The reader accepts responsibility in the use of any information and takes advice given in this book at their own risk. If the reader is under medication supervision or has had complications with health-related risks, consult your primary care physician as soon as possible before taking any advice given in this book.

The information and advice contained in this book are based upon the research and the personal and professional experiences of the author. They are not intended as a substitute for consulting with a healthcare professional. The publisher and author are not responsible for any adverse effects or consequences resulting from the use of any of the suggestions, preparations, or procedures discussed in this book. All matters pertaining to your physical health should be supervised by a healthcare professional.

ISBN: 978-93-59839-78-3
eISBN: 978-93-59838-60-1

©Author

Publisher: Pharos Books (P) Ltd.
Plot No.-55, Main Mother Dairy Road
Pandav Nagar, East Delhi-110092
Phone: 011-40395855, +4049916623
WhatsApp: +91 8368220032
E-mail: sales@pharosbooks.in
Website: www.pharosbooks.in
First Edition: 2024

I Can, I Will, I Must!
By Kevin B DiBacco

CONTENTS

Positive thinking is the rich soil, and thoughts are the seeds. When you sow well, your reality will blossom with a garden of endless possibilities. Thinking positively has a magical effect. The title "I Can, I Will, I Must" emphasizes a dedication to both professional and personal development as well as practical solutions.

In this book, scientific research and practical wisdom are expertly combined by author Kevin B. DiBacco to create a gripping story that encourages readers to realize their extraordinary potential.

This book serves as a potent reminder that each challenge presents a chance for development.

Dr. Firdous Nisar (PT),

DPT, certified, Digital Marketing and Advertising Certified, Physiotherapist at District Head Quarter Hospital Faisalabad, Pakistan. Health, Medical & Lifestyle writer.

Kevin's book, "I Can, I Will, I Must," is a powerful testament to the transformative impact of positive thinking. Through his personal journey of resilience and growth amid severe health challenges, Kevin provides practical tools for readers to navigate their own adversities.

The book not only emphasizes the effectiveness of positive thinking in overcoming obstacles but also offers actionable exercises to reshape mindset and promote well-being. Kevin's insights extend to mental and physical health, relationships, and work life, making it a comprehensive guide to a more fulfilling life.

"I Can, I Will, I Must" is not just a book; it's an inspiring roadmap for anyone seeking to embrace the strength of positive thinking and create a life filled with hope and possibility.

Dr. Barbara Harris,

Public Health Dr.

Medical Consultant/Health Writer, USA

Introduction

Kevin understands adversity and the temptation to quit better than most. His life has been a testament to the power of perseverance despite severe hardship. Now he shares his story and tools to inspire others to get off the mat when knocked down by life.

Kevin's health struggles began early, needing major surgery at just 16 years old. In his 20s and 30s, he endured 6 knee operations, 2 back surgeries including spinal fusion, 2 hip replacements, and treatment for an aggressive brain tumor. Enduring over 10 major medical procedures would be enough to make anyone want to give up. Even as he was writing this, Kevin was struck by Covid-19. As if that were not another setback, Kevin developed Pneumonia and spent the spring of 2022 and the summer of 2023 having to get daily nebulizer treatments. Once again, his theories were put to the test. Once again, they worked!

But Kevin refused to see himself as a victim of circumstance. Through each diagnosis and rehabilitation, he consciously worked to reframe adversity as an opportunity for growth. Instead of sadly ruminating on limitations, he focused positively on each small win standing, walking, climbing stairs during recovery. He visualized himself healed and happy, against all odds.

Kevin leaned on his deep faith and the support of loved ones during the darkest times. When fear or hopelessness crept in, he prayed for the strength to take the next step forward. He turned to uplifting books and sayings for encouragement. Slowly but surely, he reclaimed his active lifestyle step by step.

Through his journey, Kevin realized firsthand the power of mindset to determine one's experience of life. He discovered that by controlling his inner world through his thoughts, beliefs, visualizations, he could transform his outer reality. Now he hopes to share these lessons with others facing major life challenges.

Kevin's book recounts his medical battles, along with the techniques he used to stay grounded in positivity. He provides exercises to overcome negative self-talk, face fears, and visualize desired outcomes. Kevin believes we can all learn to reframe difficulties as growth opportunities. Wherever we feel like quitting, he urges us to proclaim, "I will keep going!"

Kevin's dramatic story provides living proof that, regardless of what knocks us down, we can choose to get back up. We all have access to inner reserves of strength to endure the unendurable. Kevin hopes his book will inspire others to fight major life battles to find their power to keep progressing. By committing to personal growth, we can overcome any obstacle, including those within our mind.

CHAPTER

1

Overview: The Power of Positive Thinking

Positive thinking is a powerful mindset that can influence our lives and contributes to our success and personal growth. It entails approaching negative situations with positive thinking and acknowledging the reality of the situation. By cultivating an optimistic mindset, we can navigate through challenges, overcome obstacles, and find opportunities for growth.

Positive thinking can shape our perception, emotions, and actions, allowing us to approach life with resilience and optimism. It plays a vital role in achieving success and personal growth by fostering a proactive and solution-oriented mindset. By maintaining a positive outlook, individuals are more likely to act, overcome challenges, and seize opportunities.

For example, consider the story of Thomas Edison, the inventor of the light bulb. Despite facing numerous failures and setbacks in his quest to create a working light bulb, Edison maintained a positive mindset. He famously said, "I have not failed. I've just found 10,000 ways that won't work." Edison's determination and positive thinking eventually led to the invention of the electric light bulb, transforming the world.

Benefits of Positive Thinking

The practice of positive thinking offers numerous benefits that can enhance our overall well-being and quality of life. One of the key advantages of positive thinking is its impact on stress management. When we maintain a positive mindset, we are better equipped to handle stress and cope with demanding situations. By approaching stressors with resilience and effective coping strategies, we can minimize their negative impact on our mental and emotional well-being. Furthermore, positive thinking has been linked to improved mental health. It lowers the risk of depression by allowing individuals to focus on the positive aspects of life and maintain an optimistic attitude. A positive mindset also promotes emotional stability, resulting in fewer mood swings and greater emotional well-being.

In addition to mental health benefits, positive thinking has a positive impact on physical health. Research has shown that individuals who maintain a positive mindset have a stronger immune system, lower blood pressure, and a decreased risk of heart disease. By reducing stress levels, positive thinking contributes to better cardiovascular health and overall physical well-being.

Another aspect of positive thinking is its influence on problem-solving skills. When faced with challenges, positive thinkers are more likely to approach them with a solution-oriented mindset. They can think creatively and find innovative ways to overcome obstacles, leading to effective decision-making and problem-solving.

Moreover, positive thinking fosters adaptability to change. By maintaining an optimistic outlook, individuals are more open to new experiences and can navigate transitions more smoothly. This adaptability allows for personal growth and the ability to embrace new opportunities.

Consider the story of Sara Blakely, the founder of Spanx. Blakely faced numerous rejections and challenges when trying to bring her innovative shape-wear concept to market. However, her positive mindset and determination allowed her to persevere. Today, Spanx is a globally recognized brand, and Blakely is a billionaire entrepreneur.

Positive Thinking and Success

Positive thinking is intricately linked to success. By cultivating a positive mindset, individuals are more likely to take action, persist in the face of obstacles, and ultimately achieve their goals. Positive thinkers view setbacks as temporary and opportunities for growth, maintaining a belief in their abilities and remaining motivated.

Numerous successful individuals attribute their achievements to positive thinking. For example, Oprah Winfrey, one of the most influential media figures in the world, emphasizes the power of positive thinking in her life. Her positive mindset has played a significant role in her success, allowing her to overcome challenges and inspire millions of people.

Likewise, Elon Musk, the CEO of SpaceX and Tesla, acknowledges the importance of positive thinking in his entrepreneurial journey. Despite facing numerous setbacks and failures, Musk maintains a positive mindset and uses each experience as an opportunity to learn and grow. His positive thinking has been instrumental in driving innovation and achieving success.

By adopting a positive mindset, individuals can enhance their problem-solving skills and approach challenges with a solution-oriented mindset. They are more likely to think creatively and find innovative solutions to problems, contributing to their success.

For instance, consider the story of Steve Jobs, the co-founder of Apple. Jobs faced numerous challenges throughout his career, including being fired from the company he helped create. However, he maintained a positive mindset and used his setbacks as opportunities for growth and innovation. His ability to think differently and embrace failure as a learning experience led to the creation of groundbreaking products that revolutionized the technology industry.

Strategies for Developing a Positive Mindset

Developing a positive mindset requires conscious effort and practice. Here are some strategies to cultivate a positive outlook and embrace the power of positive thinking:

Practicing gratitude: Take time each day to acknowledge and appreciate the positive aspects of life. This can be done through journaling or simply expressing gratitude in daily interactions. By focusing on the things, we are grateful for, we shift our mindset towards positivity and abundance.

Prioritizing self-care: Taking care of our physical and mental well-being is essential for maintaining a positive mindset. Prioritize activities such as exercise, sufficient sleep, and relaxation techniques that promote overall well-being. When we feel good physically, we are better able to maintain a positive outlook.

Accepting situations as they are: It is important to accept situations as they are and focus on what can be controlled and improved. By accepting the reality of a situation, we can direct our energy towards finding solutions and making positive changes.

Engaging in personal growth: Actively seek opportunities for personal growth and self-improvement. Identify areas where you want to grow and take steps towards achieving your goals. This growth-oriented mindset fosters positivity and allows us to continually develop ourselves.

Surrounding yourself with positivity: Surround yourself with positive influences, supportive individuals, and uplifting environments. Seek relationships and friendships that inspire and motivate you. Surrounding yourself with positivity can have a significant impact on your mindset and outlook.

Cultivating resilience: Embrace challenges as opportunities for growth and learning. Develop resilience by viewing setbacks as temporary and maintaining a belief in your ability to overcome obstacles. By cultivating resilience, you can navigate through difficulties with a positive mindset.

By incorporating these strategies into your daily life, you can develop a more positive mindset and embrace the power of positive thinking. Remember that developing a positive mindset is a journey, and it takes time and effort to change your thought patterns. Be patient and kind to yourself as you work towards cultivating a more positive outlook.

Overcoming Negative Thinking

Negative thinking can be a significant barrier to success and personal growth. It often involves filtering out positive thoughts and focusing on the negative aspects of a situation. Overcoming negative thinking is essential for developing a positive mindset and embracing the power of positive thinking.

One effective strategy for overcoming negative thinking is reframing negative situations. Instead of automatically viewing a setback as a failure, try to see it as an opportunity for growth and learning. By reframing negative situations, we can shift our perspective and find positive aspects even in challenging circumstances.

For example, suppose you didn't get a promotion at work. Instead of feeling defeated, reframe the situation by focusing on the skills and experiences you gained during the process. Use the experience as an opportunity to identify areas for growth and set new goals for professional development.

Challenging negative thoughts is another helpful strategy. When negative thoughts arise, question their validity and replace them with more positive and realistic thoughts. For instance, if you catch yourself thinking, "I'm not good enough," challenge that thought by reminding yourself of past accomplishments and strengths. Replace it with a positive affirmation, such as, "I am capable and deserving of success."

Seeking support from others can also be instrumental in overcoming negative thinking. Reach out to trusted friends, family members, or mentors who can provide a fresh perspective and offer support. They can help challenge negative beliefs and provide encouragement as you work towards developing a more positive mindset.

By consistently practicing these strategies, individuals can gradually overcome negative thinking and cultivate a more positive and optimistic outlook on life.

Examples of Positive Thinking in Action

Positive thinking manifests in various aspects of life, providing individuals with the tools to approach challenges, embrace opportunities, and achieve success. Here are some examples of positive thinking in action:

Embracing discomfort for personal growth: Positive thinkers see discomfort as a catalyst for personal growth. They willingly step out of their comfort zones, try new things, and embrace challenges. For example, someone who is afraid of public speaking may decide to join a public speaking club to overcome their fear. By embracing discomfort, they grow both personally and professionally.

Maintaining a positive outlook in challenging times: Positive thinkers maintain a hopeful attitude even during challenging times. They focus on finding solutions rather than dwelling on problems. For instance, during a difficult financial period, someone with a positive mindset may choose to explore new opportunities for income generation rather than succumbing to despair.

Approaching failure as a learning opportunity: Positive thinkers view failure as a stepping stone to success. They see it as a valuable learning experience and an opportunity to improve. For instance, an entrepreneur whose startup didn't succeed may analyze the reasons for failure, learn from the experience, and apply those lessons to future endeavors.

Positive thinking is not limited to extraordinary individuals; it is a mindset that anyone can develop and apply in their lives.

By embracing positive thinking, we can navigate through life's challenges with resilience, find opportunities for growth, and achieve success in various areas.

Positive Thinking and Personal Growth

Switching to a positive mindset can lead to significant personal growth by fostering resilience, adaptability, and a growth-oriented perspective. Positive thinking allows individuals to view obstacles as temporary setbacks and opportunities for learning. It provides the motivation, focus, and belief in one's abilities needed to achieve personal goals.

When individuals embrace positive thinking, they develop resilience—the ability to bounce back from setbacks and persevere in the face of challenges. Positive thinkers see setbacks as temporary and use them as opportunities to learn and grow. This resilience allows them to overcome obstacles and continue moving forward.

Consider the story of Malala Yousafzai, the youngest Nobel Prize laureate. Despite facing life-threatening challenges due to her advocacy for girls' education, Malala maintained a positive mindset and continued to fight for what she believed in. Her resilience and positive thinking allowed her to overcome adversity and make a significant impact on the world.

Positive thinking also fosters adaptability, which is essential for personal growth. When individuals maintain an optimistic outlook, they are more open to new experiences and can navigate transitions more smoothly. This adaptability allows for personal growth and the ability to embrace new opportunities.

Moreover, positive thinking promotes a growth-oriented perspective. When individuals believe in their abilities and maintain a positive mindset, they are more likely to take on challenges and pursue their goals. This growth-oriented mindset fuels personal development and leads to increased self-confidence and a sense of fulfillment.

For instance, consider the story of Maya Angelou, a renowned author and poet. Despite facing numerous challenges and setbacks, Angelou maintained a positive mindset and used her experiences as inspiration for her writing. Her growth-oriented perspective allowed her to continually learn, evolve, and make a profound impact on literature and society.

By embracing positive thinking, individuals can unlock their full potential and experience personal growth in various aspects of life.

Developing a Positive Attitude

Developing a positive attitude is a crucial aspect of embracing positive thinking and achieving success. A positive attitude boosts confidence, enabling individuals to take on new challenges without fear of failure. It also contributes to success by attracting opportunities, fostering productive relationships, and maintaining motivation during difficult times.

Developing a positive attitude starts with self-awareness and self-reflection. Take the time to identify negative thought patterns and beliefs that may be holding you back, and consciously work on replacing them with positive and empowering thoughts. By cultivating self-awareness, you can become more conscious of your mindset and make intentional changes to develop a positive attitude.

Surrounding yourself with positive influences is also essential for developing a positive attitude. Seek relationships and friendships that inspire and motivate you. Surround yourself with individuals who radiate positivity and share your values and goals. These positive influences can have a significant impact on your mindset and outlook.

Consider the influence of a positive mentor or role model in your life. Their positive attitude and success can inspire and motivate you to develop a similar mindset and achieve your own goals.

Cultivating a positive attitude also involves focusing on solutions rather than dwelling on problems. When faced with a challenge, positive thinkers maintain a belief in their ability to find solutions and overcome obstacles. They approach concerns with an optimistic and solution-oriented mindset, which contributes to their success.

Practical Tips for Positive Thinking

Incorporating positive thinking into daily life requires consistent effort and practice. Here are some practical tips for cultivating a positive mindset:

Replace negative thoughts with positive self-talk: Challenge negative thoughts and replace them with positive affirmations. Focus on your strengths and remind yourself of your capabilities. By consciously replacing negative thoughts with positive self-talk, you can rewire your thinking patterns and cultivate a more positive mindset.

Practice mindfulness: Engage in mindfulness practices to train your mind to think positively. Mindfulness involves being fully present in the moment without judgment. By practicing mindfulness, you can become more aware of your thoughts and emotions, allowing you to choose positive thoughts and responses.

Identify and replace negative thought patterns: Be aware of negative thought patterns and habits, and consciously work on replacing them with positive alternatives. This may involve challenging negative beliefs, reframing negative situations, and focusing on positive aspects of a situation.

Surround yourself with positive influences: Seek positive influences, such as supportive friends, mentors, and uplifting environments. Surrounding yourself with positive people and engaging in positive activities can reinforce a positive mindset.

Cultivate gratitude: Practice gratitude by keeping a gratitude journal, expressing appreciation for the positive experiences in your life, and savoring moments of joy and gratitude. By actively cultivating gratitude, you can shift your focus towards the positive aspects of life and foster a more positive mindset.

Incorporate joy and laughter: Infuse more moments of joy, playfulness, and laughter into your daily life. Engage in activities that bring you joy, spend time with loved ones who make you laugh, or watch a funny movie or comedy show. Laughter and joy have a positive impact on your mood and overall well-being.

By incorporating these practical tips into your daily life, you can develop a more positive mindset and embrace the power of positive thinking. Remember that developing a positive attitude is a journey that requires consistent effort and practice. Be patient and kind to yourself as you work towards cultivating a more positive outlook.

Embracing the Power of Positive Thinking

Positive thinking is a powerful tool that can transform every aspect of our lives. By adopting a positive mindset, we can enhance our well-being, strengthen our problem-solving skills, and achieve success in various areas. Embracing positive thinking allows us to navigate through challenges with resilience, find opportunities for growth, and experience personal fulfillment.

Throughout history, numerous individuals have demonstrated the power of positive thinking in their lives. From Thomas Edison to Oprah Winfrey, their stories serve as inspiration for us to cultivate a positive mindset and achieve our own goals.

Remember, developing a positive mindset is a continuous journey that requires conscious effort and practice. It may not always be easy, but the rewards are immense. By embracing positive thinking and incorporating practical strategies into our daily lives, we can unleash our full potential and create a brighter future.

The roots of positive thinking can be traced back thousands of years to the ancient wisdom traditions and philosophical schools of thought in China, India, Greece, and Egypt. Concepts related to positive thinking emerged both as a philosophical approach to life and as a prescription for health and wellbeing.

Some of the earliest origins of positive thinking philosophically can be found in ancient Chinese Taoist and Confucian teachings. Taoism promoted the concept of going with the flow, being flexible, and finding positivity and opportunity within every situation. Confucian teachings focused on self-improvement, self-cultivation, and optimistically striving to reach one's potential. These schools of thought advised looking inward to find positivity and exercising agency to create a happy life.

In ancient India, schools of thought like Vedanta Hinduism and Buddhism promoted similar positive perspectives. Hindu texts emphasized one's power to shape reality through positive thinking and intention. Core concepts like karma taught that positivity breeds positivity. Buddhism stressed the importance of training one's mind, shaping one's perspective of events, and focusing on happiness arising from within. Practices like yoga and meditation were developed to cultivate positivity.

In Ancient Greece, the philosophies of Stoicism and Platonism would shape early Western positive thinking. Stoicism taught that happiness results from having an attitude aligned with the natural order of events. The philosophy advised training one's mind to remain calm, disciplined, and positive in the face of adversity. Plato's philosophy also held optimism and belief in a fundamental order of the universe. Happiness and harmony would come from discovering and living in truth with this universal order.

Psychologists often credit the New Thought movement in America in the 19th century as the beginning of positive thinking as a self-help philosophy. Figures like Phineas Quimby, Ralph Waldo Emerson, and William James pioneered this philosophy, which held that spiritual and mental attitudes shape tangible realities. Mind over matter and the power of intention were core principles. New Thought paved the way for new spiritual movements emphasizing health and prosperity through positive minds, including Christian Science, New Thought, and Unity Church.

The late 19th and early 20th centuries saw the emergence of new schools of positive psychology in America and Europe. William James, called the "father" of American psychology, championed the study of healthy mindedness and human happiness. In Europe, a French pharmacist turned psychologist, Émile Coué, promoted "conscious autosuggestion" and the mantra "Every day, in every way, I am getting better and better."

But it was perhaps Norman Vincent Peale who brought positive thinking into the American mainstream. His 1952 book The Power of Positive Thinking became a national bestseller and fueled the rise of positive thinking in self-help culture and business motivation. Peale, an author and minister, believed positive visualizations and affirmations could align one's life with God's grand plan.

Modern positive psychology again pushed positive thinking into the realm of social science. Pioneered by psychologists like Martin Seligman in the 1990s, positive psychology uses empirical research to study human virtues, strengths, optimism, and happiness. Practices like cognitive behavioral therapy are grounded in training one's thoughts and self-talk to be more positive.

Today, positive thinking has permeated popular culture, business leadership, sports coaching, and everyday self-help practices. Millions subscribe to daily positive thinking and affirmation practices to reduce stress, overcome challenges, and work toward goals. Apps, books, seminars, and speakers on positive thinking abound as both individuals and organizations aim to harness its benefits.

At its core, positive thinking emerges from a simple belief that our mindset and attitude shape our realities, health, relationships, and achievement of goals. By monitoring thoughts and speech and exercising agency over one's perspective, we can optimize our mindsets. This builds resilience, motivation, creativity, and wellbeing to reach our full potential. While positive thinking alone cannot solve all problems, its intent is to maximize one's capacity to thrive and steer life in a positive direction.

How Positive Thinking Will Change Your Life

The power of positive thinking is immense and can truly transform a person's life in profound ways, both mentally and physically. Adopting a mindset of optimism, hope, and focusing on the bright side of life allows a person to approach the world from a perspective of possibility rather than limitation. This opens opportunities, fuels motivation, and allows one to envision goals and take the actions necessary to achieve them.

On a mental level, positive thinking can improve overall happiness and life satisfaction. It enables a person to appreciate what they have rather than dwelling on what they lack. With a positive outlook, people can see setbacks as temporary challenges rather than permanent failures, which protects against depression and despair. Thinking positively also boosts confidence and self-esteem, as people give themselves credit for successes instead of blaming external factors. This empowers people to pursue their dreams and handle adversity in a healthy, constructive way.

Positive thinking not only mitigates negative emotions like stress, anger, and sadness, but also enhances positive emotions like joy, gratitude, and contentment. This creates a feedback loop where positive thoughts lead to positive feelings, which in turn lead to more positive thoughts. Over time, this process can rewire the brain's neural pathways to become more inclined towards optimism and happiness. Intentionally adopting a positive perspective also opens people up to notice and appreciate the goodness in their lives, whereas chronic negativity can blind people to the positive experiences they have each day.

In terms of physical health, positive thinking has been shown to strengthen the immune system, lower blood pressure, and reduce pain sensitivity. A positive mindset is associated with healthier behaviors like exercising, eating well, and getting adequate sleep. Optimistic people tend to have an internal locus of control and believe their actions have an impact, which motivates them to actively care for their health through positive lifestyle habits. Positivity may also benefit cardiovascular health by mitigating the harmful effects of stress on the heart and blood vessels.

Studies show optimists have better health outcomes when facing major illnesses like cancer. Positive thinking gives patients motivation to follow treatment plans, the will to fight their disease, and the ability to envision their recovery. A constructive attitude also helps patients manage stress and anxiety during difficult treatments. Doctors emphasize that while positive thinking alone cannot cure illness, it significantly empowers patients and complements medical care.

For mental health disorders like depression and anxiety, positive thinking is an effective complement to professional treatment plans. Reframing negative thought patterns and intentionally developing a more hopeful mindset counteracts the pessimism that feeds disorders like depression. Looking for the bright side and focusing on strengths provides an antidote to the distorted, negative thinking that accompanies mental illness. Positive thinking habits help sufferers push back against their condition and prevents relapse by teaching self-compassion and resilience.

However, experts caution that positive thinking is not a cure-all or a replacement for professional help. It should complement medical and mental health treatment plans, not substitute them.

Severe conditions need to be managed appropriately, and positive thinking alone is not enough. But in combination with traditional care, it can be a powerful force for healing and growth.

When it comes to relationships and social life, positive thinking improves both the ability to form connections and the quality of those connections. A positive attitude makes people more charismatic, likable, and engaging. It enables people to be more open, friendly, and interested in others, rather than self-centered or withdrawn. With optimism, people see relationships as opportunities for mutual growth and support, rather than potential disappointments. These foster satisfying, enduring social bonds. Positivity also allows people to be less judgmental and more understanding of others' flaws, strengthening relationships.

In the workplace, positive thinking enhances both performance and enjoyment. Optimistic employees see tasks as opportunities and are confident in their abilities, which translates to higher productivity. A constructive attitude also helps people persist through challenges, handle criticism, and bounce back from setbacks. Workers who think positively experience less stress, frustration, and burnout. They are satisfied with their roles and feel appreciated, taking more pride in excellent work. Companies with cultures of positivity have higher employee retention rates.

For students of all ages, positive thinking helps academic performance by boosting motivation, engagement, and self-esteem. Envisioning success rather than failure becomes a self-fulfilling prophecy. A positive attitude helps students handle challenges like difficult material, competitive environments, and heavy workloads. It also fosters effective study habits, time management skills, and collaborative relationships. Most importantly, optimism helps students believe in their abilities, so they reach their potential.

Spiritually, positive thinking helps people find meaning and purpose. Optimists are more likely to feel connected to something larger than themselves or a higher power. A constructive perspective allows people to be open to inspiration, find blessings in challenges, and align their actions with their values. Positivity gives people faith in overcoming adversity and empowers them to have a growth mindset throughout life's journey. With optimism, people feel called to meaningful contributions that improve the world.

While there are many more ways positive thinking powerfully transforms lives, the main takeaway is that an optimistic mindset fills people with hopefulness for the future and belief in themselves. Though staying positive takes practice, it enables people to envision goals, pursue growth, overcome challenges, build connections, care for their health, and find meaning. By making mental shifts towards gratitude, confidence, and kindness, anyone can harness the strength of positive thinking to create their best life.

In our quest for a better life, positive thinking serves as a powerful tool that enables us to overcome the greatest of challenges. In my life, positive thinking has played a transformative role in helping me navigate through the trials of brain surgery, brain radiation, back and hip surgeries. Through these experiences, I have witnessed firsthand the remarkable impact of positive thinking in overcoming adversity and finding strength in the face of immense difficulties.

Unlocking Opportunities through Perception: Throughout my medical journey, positive thinking became my guiding light. When faced with the daunting prospect of brain surgery, I chose to view it as an opportunity for healing and growth rather than succumbing to fear. By maintaining a positive outlook, I approached the procedure with a sense of resilience and determination, believing that I could emerge stronger on the other side.

Building Resilience and Adaptability: Brain surgery, brain radiation, and subsequent back and hip surgeries presented a series of challenges that tested my resilience. Through positive thinking, I fostered an unwavering belief in my ability to adapt and overcome these obstacles. It was through this mindset that I found the strength to persevere, even when the road seemed insurmountable. Positive thinking instilled within me the courage to face each surgery with optimism and the conviction that I could navigate the recovery process with determination and grace.

Enhancing Emotional Well-being: The impact of positive thinking on my emotional well-being cannot be overstated. In the face of medical procedures and the subsequent recovery periods, maintaining a positive mindset allowed me to find solace amidst the physical and emotional pain. By focusing on the potential for healing and the lessons I could learn from each experience, I cultivated a sense of inner peace and gratitude. This emotional resilience supported my well-being and had a profound impact on those around me, creating an environment of hope and encouragement.

Igniting the Drive to Overcome: Positive thinking became the driving force behind my determination to overcome the hurdles I faced. Through every surgery and recovery, I kept my sights set on my goals, constantly reminding myself of the possibilities that lay ahead. Positive thinking fueled my motivation to regain my strength and mobility, enabling me to push through the difficult moments and celebrate even the smallest victories along the way.

The Ripple Effect on Health: Positive thinking became an integral part of my healing journey. By maintaining a positive mindset, I experienced reduced stress levels and an enhanced sense of well-being, which directly impacted my physical health. It allowed me to approach my rehabilitation exercises with dedication and a belief in the healing power of my body. Positive thinking played a vital role in my recovery process, enabling me to regain strength, mobility, and ultimately reclaim my life.

My personal journey of conquering brain surgery, brain radiation, back and hip surgeries stands as a testament to the transformative power of positive thinking. It illuminated a path of triumph through the darkest times, unlocking opportunities, building resilience, enhancing emotional well-being, and igniting an unwavering drive to overcome. Not only did positive thinking transform my life, but it also inspired those around me. As we embark on our respective journeys, let us embrace the incredible strength that lies within us, recognizing that positive thinking holds the power to overcome any adversity and thrive. Let us embrace this remarkable tool and allow it to guide us towards a life of triumph and limitless possibilities.

CHAPTER

2

Shifting your mindset

The Key Principles to the Art of 'Positive Thinking'

Positive thinking is a mindset that focuses on constructive and optimistic perspectives. Here are five key principles of positive thinking and a brief overview of the theory:

1. **Optimism**: Positive thinkers tend to see the glass as half full rather than half empty. They believe that positive outcomes are possible even in challenging situations.

2. **Positive Self-Talk**: This involves replacing negative self-talk with positive and encouraging thoughts. It's about being kind and supportive to oneself.

3. **Resilience**: Positive thinkers are often more resilient in the face of adversity. They see setbacks as temporary and opportunities for growth.

4. **Gratitude**: Practicing gratitude involves acknowledging and appreciating the good things in life. It can help shift the focus from what's lacking to what's present.

5. **Visualization**: Positive thinkers regularly use visualization techniques to imagine their goals and desired outcomes. This can help reinforce their belief in achieving these goals.

The theory behind positive thinking suggests that our thoughts and attitudes have a significant impact on our emotions, behaviors, and outcomes. By maintaining a positive mindset, individuals can improve their overall well-being and increase their chances of achieving success and happiness. This theory is typically associated with the field of positive psychology, which explores the science of happiness and human flourishing.

Part I: Your Mindset

Cultivating a Growth Mindset: Embracing a mindset of continuous learning and improvement.

The importance of believing in your ability to change and develop new skills.

Strategies to overcome self-limiting beliefs and embrace challenges.

Gratitude and Appreciation: Harnessing the transformative power of gratitude.

Practicing gratitude as a daily habit and its positive impact on mental and emotional well-being.

Techniques for cultivating gratitude in challenging situations.

Reframing Negative Thoughts: Transforming negative thinking patterns into positive ones.

Recognizing common cognitive distortions and challenging negative self-talk.

Tools and exercises to reframe negative thoughts and create a positive perspective.

Part II: Nurturing a Positive Lifestyle

Self-Compassion and Self-Acceptance: Embracing kindness and forgiveness towards oneself.

The importance of self-compassion in building resilience and maintaining a positive outlook.

Practices and techniques for cultivating self-acceptance.

Surrounding Yourself with Positivity: Creating an environment that supports positive thinking.

Identifying toxic influences and cultivating relationships that nurture positivity.

Strategies for fostering positivity in the workplace, social circles, and personal life.

Mindfulness and Present Moment Awareness: Being fully present to experience joy and peace.

The benefits of mindfulness in reducing stress, enhancing focus, and increasing happiness.

Practical exercises to cultivate mindfulness and live in the present moment.

Part III: Taking Action and Achieving Success

Setting Goals and Visualizing Success: Using the power of intention to manifest your desires.

The importance of setting clear, achievable goals and creating a vision for success.

Techniques for visualizing success and using positive affirmations to reinforce beliefs.

Overcoming Obstacles and Building Resilience: Embracing challenges as opportunities for growth.

Strategies to overcome setbacks, bounce back from failure, and build resilience.

Developing a positive mindset in the face of adversity and staying motivated.

Taking Inspired Action: Turning positive thoughts into tangible results.

The role of inspired action in manifesting goals and dreams.

Practical steps to take action, stay motivated, and persevere towards success.

The lifelong practice of positive thinking and its transformative effects on personal and professional life.

When Reality hits

That feeling when your heart sinks into your stomach.

You can't just talk about positive thinking without having used it in your life. I have been told by many doctors that without my attitude, I would be sitting in a wheelchair by now. All my doctors acknowledge that my thinking and work ethic has put me far ahead of others going through what I did at the time. Having sports surgeries early in life, I knew what it took to get back into proper health. As the surgeries piled up, I developed a mindset to get back to health in the minimum time. That all worked fine until I had brain surgery.

While watching the NFL playoffs, I believe it was the Patriots/Steelers at my sister's one evening, my right eye started to go blurry. I thought I was just tired. I stayed the night there and went home the next morning. Not only that, but I noticed that my right eye was still blurry. Once I got home, I talked to Rachel and said something happened to my eye. We agreed that I should call the doctor. My PC said, since you just had back surgery a few years before, schedule an appointment with your neurosurgeon. That day I will never forget.

We headed to his office, and we were lucky to get right in. He looked into my eyes, took a few x-rays and while we waited in his office, Dr. F came in with a handful of x-rays, not smiling. He said, Well, Kev, we have a problem." He slides the x-rays on the wall viewer and with his grease pencil circles a big white mass right in the middle of my head. Cracking a joke, he says this should not be here! I looked at Rachel, who had a shocked look on her face. 'Oh Shit' I said, that's not like back surgery. Dr. F laughed and said no, this is like 5 back surgeries in one. We sat and talked. He assured me that he has done many of these. I had a one-half inch mass sitting on my right optic nerve. The problem was that it was attached to my pituitary gland. That's when he told me the odds of survival and the odds of losing your sight. Neither one was in my favor. He prepared me for what was going to happen. He had his nurses call me once I got home and set up the surgery about 2 months later. The concern was: I only had one eye, and I had just finished shooting a low-budget movie that I had to edit! For two months, I literally lived with one eye. I actually edited and finished the movie with one eye, and it was sold to a worldwide distributor. On a side note, I also had to renew my driver's license. So I trekked on down to the DMV, fully expecting to flunk the eye exam. I had my papers from the doctor, thinking I may need a waiver. I did not say a word and took the test. Pretty much guessing what the right eye letters were. She said ok, good! "What," she said, good to go. I said huh, I woke up with this infection or something in my eye, that's surprising. The DMV lady laughed and looked me in the eye laughing. " You only require one eye to drive"... We both laughed, and I knew that this would be an adventure!!

The odds of not making it through back or hip surgery are on your side. Once I was told by my neurosurgeons that the odds of brain surgery were much lower. A 10-hour surgery and anything can go wrong. I would need to brush up on all my past positive thinking techniques. Not for just the surgery, but for the two years following. Hormone therapies, weekly blood tests, MRI's, eye exams, kidney tests. This was the real deal and I had to get ready!

How I tested Positive Thinking in my real-life situations

Massive back surgery

Undergoing back surgery that results in lifetime nerve damage can have significant emotional and physical impacts on an individual's life. Here are some common issues that people may face in such situations:

Emotional Issues: Chronic pain: Nerve damage can lead to chronic pain, which can be debilitating and impact one's emotional well-being. Dealing with constant or recurring pain can lead to frustration, anxiety, depression, and a decreased quality of life.

Emotional distress: Coping with the long-term effects of nerve damage can cause emotional distress. This may include feelings of sadness, grief, anger, or frustration due to the loss of physical function or the inability to engage in activities that were once enjoyable.

Adjustment to limitations: Nerve damage can result in limitations in mobility, strength, and overall physical functioning. Adjusting to these limitations may require significant lifestyle changes, such as avoiding certain activities, using assistive devices, or relying on others for assistance. Adapting to these changes can be emotionally challenging and may require time to process and accept.

Loss of independence: Nerve damage can affect one's ability to perform daily tasks independently. This loss of independence can be emotionally distressing and may lead to feelings of helplessness, dependence, and a sense of burden on others.

Anxiety and fear: Nerve damage and the associated symptoms can cause anxiety and fear about the future, such as concerns about worsening pain, potential complications, or the need for additional surgeries or treatments. These anxieties can contribute to emotional distress and impact on overall well-being.

Physical Issues: Chronic pain: Nerve damage often leads to chronic pain, which can be severe and persistent. The pain may radiate along the affected nerves and can be challenging to manage, even with medication and other pain management techniques.

Sensory and motor deficits: Nerve damage can result in sensory changes, such as numbness, tingling, or hypersensitivity in the affected area. It can also cause motor deficits, leading to muscle weakness, loss of coordination, or difficulty with fine motor skills.

Loss of function: Nerve damage may result in a loss of function in the affected areas. This can impact mobility, balance, and the ability to perform certain activities or tasks.

Rehabilitation challenges: Physical rehabilitation and therapy may be required to maximize function and manage pain after back surgery with nerve damage. However, nerve damage can pose challenges to the effectiveness of rehabilitation efforts, making it more difficult to achieve desired outcomes.

Impaired quality of life: The physical limitations and ongoing pain associated with nerve damage can significantly impact an individual's overall quality of life. Everyday activities, hobbies, and social interactions may be impacted, leading to a decreased sense of well-being and satisfaction.

It's important for individuals dealing with lifetime nerve damage after back surgery to seek support from healthcare professionals, such as pain management specialists, physical therapists, and mental health professionals. They can provide guidance, pain management strategies, rehabilitation plans, and emotional support to help navigate the challenges associated with the condition. Support groups and connecting with others who have experienced similar situations can also be beneficial in coping with the emotional and physical issues related to nerve damage.

Recovering from Brain Surgery

Undergoing brain surgery followed by brain radiation can be a challenging and emotionally taxing experience. Here are some factors that can contribute to the difficulty of this process:

Physical challenges: Brain surgery is a major medical procedure that involves the removal of brain tissue or the placement of devices or implants. It can result in physical pain, discomfort, and a period of recovery that may include restrictions on activities and medications. Brain radiation, while a non-invasive treatment, can also cause side effects such as fatigue, hair loss, skin irritation, and changes in cognitive function.

Emotional impact: Dealing with a brain surgery diagnosis and undergoing radiation treatment can have a significant emotional impact. Feelings of fear, anxiety, uncertainty, and sadness are common during this time. The uncertainty surrounding the outcome and the potential impact on cognitive abilities or quality of life can be distressing.

Lifestyle adjustments: Recovery from brain surgery and radiation may require making significant lifestyle adjustments. This can include changes in daily routines, limitations on physical activity, adjustments to work or school schedules, and potential challenges in maintaining relationships or social activities.

Long-term effects: Depending on the nature of the surgery and radiation treatment, there may be long-term effects to consider. These can include changes in cognitive abilities, memory problems, emotional changes, and potential impacts on physical functioning. Adjusting to these changes and managing their effects can be challenging.

Support system: Having a strong support system, including family, friends, and healthcare professionals, can make a significant difference in coping with the challenges of brain surgery and radiation. However, the lack of adequate support can add to the difficulty of the experience.

It's important to remember that everyone's experience is unique, and individual factors such as the type and extent of the surgery, overall health, and personal resilience can influence the difficulty of the process. It's crucial to work closely with your healthcare team to ensure proper support, manage any complications, and address any concerns you may have during your recovery journey. They can provide specific guidance based on your situation and offer resources for support and rehabilitation.

Brain Radiation 5 Years After Brain Surgery

Recovering from brain radiation treatment requires a combination of physical and mental resilience. While there are no specific "mind powers" involved, certain psychological factors can contribute to a successful recovery. Here are some aspects that can help during the process:

Positive mindset: Maintaining a positive outlook can be beneficial for both physical and mental healing. Believing in your ability to recover and focusing on the positive aspects of your life can improve your overall well-being.

Resilience and determination: Facing the challenges associated with brain radiation treatment requires resilience. It involves staying committed to the treatment plan, coping with side effects, and pushing through difficult moments.

Emotional support: Having a strong support system, including family, friends, and healthcare professionals, can provide the emotional support needed during recovery. Sharing your feelings and seeking assistance when needed can be vital for maintaining mental well-being.

Stress management: Radiation treatment and its side effects can be stressful. Developing effective stress management techniques such as deep breathing exercises, meditation, mindfulness, or engaging in activities you enjoy can help reduce stress levels.

Patience and self-compassion: Recovery from brain radiation treatment takes time, and it's important to be patient with yourself. Being kind to yourself, practicing self-care, and acknowledging your progress, no matter how small, can contribute to a healthier mindset.

Seeking professional help: If you find it challenging to cope with the emotional and psychological impact of brain radiation treatment, consider seeking support from mental health professionals. They can provide guidance, therapy, or counseling to help you navigate through the recovery process.

It's worth noting that each individual's experience and recovery journey may vary. It's essential to consult your healthcare team, including radiation oncologists and other specialists, who can provide personalized advice and support based on your specific circumstances.

Undergoing brain surgery followed by brain radiation can be a challenging and emotionally taxing experience. Here are some factors that can contribute to the difficulty of this process:

Physical challenges: Brain surgery is a major medical procedure that involves the removal of brain tissue or the placement of devices or implants. It can result in physical pain, discomfort, and a period of recovery that may include restrictions on activities and medications. Brain radiation, while a non-invasive treatment, can also cause side effects such as fatigue, hair loss, skin irritation, and changes in cognitive function.

Emotional impact: Dealing with a brain surgery diagnosis and undergoing radiation treatment can have a significant emotional impact. Feelings of fear, anxiety, uncertainty, and sadness are common during this time. The uncertainty surrounding the outcome and the potential impact on cognitive abilities or quality of life can be distressing.

Lifestyle adjustments: Recovery from brain surgery and radiation may require making significant lifestyle adjustments. This can include changes in daily routines, limitations on physical activity, adjustments to work or school schedules, and potential challenges in maintaining relationships or social activities.

Long-term effects: Depending on the nature of the surgery and radiation treatment, there may be long-term effects to consider. These can include changes in cognitive abilities, memory problems, emotional changes, and potential impacts on physical functioning. Adjusting to these changes and managing their effects can be challenging.

Support system: Having a strong support system, including family, friends, and healthcare professionals, can make a significant difference in coping with the challenges of brain surgery and radiation. However, the lack of adequate support can add to the difficulty of the experience.

It's important to remember that everyone's experience is unique, and individual factors such as the type and extent of the surgery, overall health, and personal resilience can influence the difficulty of the process. It's crucial to work closely with your healthcare team to ensure proper support, manage any complications, and address any concerns you may have during your recovery journey. They can provide specific guidance based on your situation and offer resources for support and rehabilitation.

Double Hip Surgery Recovery

Undergoing a double hip replacement surgery can result in various emotional and physical stresses. Here are some common challenges individuals may face during the process:

Physical pain and discomfort: Following double hip replacement surgery, patients often experience significant pain and discomfort in the hip and surrounding areas. This discomfort can persist during the initial recovery period, which may involve limited mobility and the use of assistive devices like crutches or walkers.

Limited mobility and independence: The recovery process after double hip replacement typically requires a period of restricted movement and rehabilitation. This can lead to temporary limitations in mobility and a reduced ability to perform daily activities independently, which can be frustrating and emotionally challenging.

Rehabilitation and physical therapy: Physical therapy is a crucial part of the recovery process. It involves exercises and movements aimed at rebuilding strength, improving range of motion, and restoring function in the hips. However, physical therapy can be physically demanding and requires dedication and effort, which may be emotionally draining.

Adaptation to lifestyle changes: Double hip replacement surgery often necessitates making adjustments to one's lifestyle. This can include modifying daily routines, avoiding certain activities that put stress on the hips, and possibly requiring the use of assistive devices for a period of time. Adapting to these changes can be emotionally difficult and may require patience and support.

Dependency and support needs: During the initial stages of recovery, individuals may require assistance with daily tasks, such as dressing, bathing, and household chores. This dependency on others can lead to feelings of vulnerability, loss of independence, and emotional stress. Having a support system in place is crucial to help manage these challenges.

Emotional and psychological impact: Going through a major surgical procedure like double hip replacement can be emotionally overwhelming. Feelings of anxiety, fear, frustration, and sadness are common during the recovery period. Coping with these emotions and maintaining a positive outlook can be challenging.

Extended recovery period: It's important to recognize that the recovery from double hip replacement surgery is a gradual process. It can take several weeks or even months to fully regain mobility, strength, and function. The prolonged recovery period can sometimes lead to feelings of impatience, frustration, and discouragement.

It's essential to communicate openly with your healthcare team, including surgeons, physical therapists, and other professionals, to address any concerns or challenges you may be experiencing. They can provide guidance, support, and appropriate resources to help manage the emotional and physical stresses associated with double hip replacement surgery.

I not only practiced the art of Positive thinking, NLP and Visualization, I had to do it multiple times within a 6-year span. Trust me, it works.

The Concept of the Brain Healing the Body is Called Neuroplasticity

Neuroplasticity is a fundamental concept in neuroscience that refers to the brain's ability to change and adapt structurally and functionally in response to experiences, learning, and environmental stimuli. It challenges the traditional belief that the brain is fixed and unchangeable after a certain age.

There are two main types of neuroplasticity: synaptic plasticity and structural plasticity. Synaptic plasticity involves changes in the strength and efficiency of connections between neurons (synapses). This process allows for the modification of existing neural networks and the formation of new connections. Structural plasticity, on the other hand, involves physical changes in the brain's structure, including the growth of new neurons (neurogenesis), the formation of new dendritic branches, and the remodeling of neural circuits.

Neuroplasticity plays a crucial role in learning, memory formation, and recovery from brain injuries. When we learn new information or acquire new skills, the connections between neurons are strengthened, and new connections may be formed. This enables the brain to reorganize its neural pathways and optimize the processing of information related to the specific task or knowledge being learned. As a result, repeated practice and exposure lead to improved performance and increased efficiency in the associated brain regions.

In terms of brain injuries or neurological conditions, neuroplasticity offers the potential for recovery and rehabilitation. When certain brain areas are damaged, other parts of the brain can compensate by taking on the functions of the affected regions or by rewiring neural connections. This rewiring allows individuals to regain lost functions or develop alternative strategies to overcome limitations. For example, after a stroke, the unaffected areas of the brain can reorganize and take over the functions that were previously handled by the damaged regions.

Numerous studies have demonstrated the remarkable effects of neuroplasticity. For instance, research has shown that individuals with visual impairments can develop enhanced tactile or auditory processing abilities due to the brain's adaptive mechanisms.

Additionally, studies have indicated that intensive and targeted training can lead to structural changes in specific brain regions. For example, London taxi drivers, who undergo extensive training to navigate the city's complex road network, have been found to have larger hippocampi (a brain region involved in spatial navigation and memory) compared to the general population.

In the field of rehabilitation, neuroplasticity-based interventions have shown promising results. For instance, in stroke patients, intensive physical therapy and repetitive motor exercises can promote the reorganization of neural pathways and improve motor function. Similarly, in individuals with neurodegenerative diseases like Parkinson's or Alzheimer's, cognitive training exercises can help maintain cognitive abilities and slow down the progression of cognitive decline.

Dr. Norman Doidge has traveled around the world and met people who have healed themselves by utilizing neuroplasticity, which is the brain's ability to change and adapt in response to experiences and stimuli. He believes that this concept could revolutionize the way we treat various conditions, from ADD to Parkinson's disease.

Neuroplasticity is a groundbreaking discovery in modern science that reveals the brain's remarkable capacity to change and heal itself. Unlike what was previously believed, the brain is not fixed and unchangeable. It can form new neural pathways to accommodate its needs. This has sparked significant interest in brain training to enhance focus, memory, attention, and performance.

In 2007, Dr. Norman Doidge gained attention with his bestseller "The Brain That Changes Itself," which brought neuroplasticity into the spotlight. Since then, he has explored the therapeutic potential of neuroplasticity and demonstrated that the brain possesses its own unique healing abilities. His latest book, "The Brain's Way of Healing: Remarkable Discoveries and Recoveries

From the Frontiers of Neuroplasticity," shares stories of patients who have successfully healed their brains without medication or surgery, focusing on conditions like multiple sclerosis, Parkinson's disease, autism, and attention deficit disorder.

In these conditions, the brain's overall neuronal and cellular health becomes disrupted due to factors such as inflammation, toxicity, or genetic abnormalities. Circuits in the brain may become inactive, die, or fire irregularly, resulting in what Doidge calls a "noisy brain." For instance, individuals with traumatic brain injury experience limitations due to dormant circuits but also hyperactivity in certain circuits, leading to heightened sensitivity to stimuli like sound and light. To rebalance the brain, a process of rest and learning is required.

Doidge describes non-invasive interventions in his book that use the senses or body movements to access the brain's healing potential. One example is the story of John Pepper, who had Parkinson's disease and did not respond well to conventional medication. By paying close attention to the individual movements involved in walking during a fitness program, Pepper discovered that he could perform those movements with heightened awareness. This was possible because the specific brain functions related to walking were still intact in Parkinson's patients. By stimulating dormant circuitry in his brain through deliberate exercises, Pepper experienced remarkable improvement in his Parkinson's symptoms.

Doidge emphasizes the accessibility of neuroplasticity, as anyone can tap into this inherent capability. The book also highlights the significance of movement, even simple acts like walking, for both the body and the brain. In fact, a study by the Cochrane Institute in Wales demonstrated that five activities—exercise, not smoking, moderate alcohol consumption, a diet rich in fruits and vegetables, and maintaining a healthy weight—reduce the risk of developing dementia by 60%. Exercise, in particular, emerged as the most influential factor.

The book also explores the relationship between pain and neuroplasticity. There are two types of pain: acute pain, which warns against further damaging a body part, and chronic pain. While acute pain is necessary for protection, chronic pain can result from neuroplastic changes in the pain system itself. Even small movements can trigger widespread and long-lasting pain. Dr. Doidge recounts the story of Dr. Michael Moskowitz, a pain physician and psychiatrist who suffered from chronic pain after multiple accidents. Moskowitz used the knowledge of brain plasticity to his advantage. Recognizing that several brain regions process both pain and other functions like emotional regulation or visualization, he focused on visualizing whenever he experienced pain. By retraining his brain through mental interventions, Moskowitz successfully overcame his chronic pain.

Doidge acknowledges that the stories of healing he presents may seem miraculous, but he emphasizes that they are based on frontier research in neuroplasticity. It is not a matter of belief or placebo effect but rather the training of new brain circuitry. Doidge encourages a scientific attitude of open-minded skepticism, urging people to explore these possibilities rather than dismissing them outright.

Overall, the concept of neuroplasticity has revolutionized our understanding of the brain's capacity to change and adapt throughout life. It offers hope for the development of innovative therapies and interventions to enhance learning, promote recovery from brain injuries, and improve the quality of life for individuals with neurological conditions.

ACTUAL CASE STUDIES THAT SUPPORT NEUROPLASTICITY

London taxi drivers: In a notable study conducted by researchers at University College London, it was found that London taxi drivers, who must pass a rigorous examination known as "The Knowledge" to obtain a license, exhibited significant structural changes in their brains. The study used MRI scans to compare the brains of taxi drivers with those of control subjects. The results strongly suggested that the taxi drivers had a larger posterior hippocampus, a region associated with spatial navigation and memory, suggesting that their brains had undergone neuroplastic changes to accommodate their extensive navigation training.

Stroke rehabilitation: Neuroplasticity has been demonstrated in stroke rehabilitation, where individuals relearn skills lost due to damage to the brain caused by a stroke. For example, a study published in the journal Neurorehabilitation and Neural Repair described the case of a patient who had lost the ability to move his right arm after a stroke. Through intensive physical therapy and task-specific exercises, the patient experienced significant improvements in motor function over time. Neuroimaging scans revealed changes in the activation patterns of the brain, indicating that the undamaged areas of the brain were able to adapt and take over the functions of the damaged regions.

Learning to play a musical instrument: Learning to play a musical instrument provides another compelling case for neuroplasticity. A study published in the Journal of Neuroscience examined the brains of professional musicians and found that they had larger areas of the motor cortex associated with finger movements compared to non-musicians. These structural differences were attributed to the extensive training and practice that musicians undergo, demonstrating how the brain can adapt and reorganize itself to master complex skills. Additionally, studies have shown that even short-term musical training can lead to neuroplastic changes in the brain, such as increased gray matter volume in areas related to auditory processing and motor control.

Stroke Rehabilitation: A study published in the New England Journal of Medicine reported a case of a 71-year-old woman who experienced a severe stroke that left her with limited movement and sensation in her left arm and hand. She participated in a rehabilitation program focused on constraint-induced movement therapy (CIMT), which involved restraining the unaffected arm and encouraging intensive use of the affected arm. Over time, the patient's brain underwent structural changes, and functional MRI scans revealed increased activation in the motor areas associated with the affected arm. As a result of the neuroplastic changes, the patient experienced substantial improvement in motor function and regained the ability to perform daily activities.

Phantom Limb Pain: Phantom limb pain is a condition where individuals experience persistent pain in a limb that has been amputated. In a case study published in the journal Nature, a patient with phantom limb pain underwent mirror therapy, a technique that uses visual illusions to alleviate the pain. By reflecting the image of the intact limb in a mirror, the brain is tricked into perceiving movement and stimulation in the amputated limb. Over time, the patient experienced a reduction in phantom limb pain, indicating that neuroplastic changes occurred in the brain to modulate the perception of pain.

Rehabilitation after Traumatic Brain Injury: A case study published in the journal Frontiers in Human Neuroscience reported on a patient who sustained a severe traumatic brain injury resulting in significant cognitive impairments. The patient underwent an intensive cognitive rehabilitation program focused on retraining attention, memory, and executive functions. Through targeted interventions and repetitive practice, the patient's brain underwent neuroplastic changes, leading to improvements in cognitive abilities. Functional MRI scans showed increased activation in the relevant brain regions, indicating successful brain reorganization.

THE GOOD NEWS: It is possible for your brain to heal.

Some believe that understanding all the processes of the brain may always remain a challenge. However, there is evidence supporting the existence of one crucial process known as neuroplasticity.

Neuroplasticity refers to the brain's ability to restructure and rewire itself when it recognizes the need for adaptation. In other words, it can continue developing and changing throughout life. For example, if a brain injury from a car accident affects your ability to speak, it doesn't necessarily mean you have permanently lost this skill. Therapy and rehabilitation can help your brain relearn it by repairing old pathways or creating new ones. Neuroplasticity also shows promise as a potential treatment approach for certain mental health conditions.

Experts believe that disrupted, or impaired neuroplasticity processes may contribute to negative thought patterns associated with conditions like depression. Engaging in exercises that promote positive neuroplasticity can potentially "rewrite" these patterns and improve overall well-being. Although rewiring the brain may sound complex, it is something you can do from the comfort of your home.

Engagement in video games: Contrary to popular belief, video games can have cognitive benefits. Research suggests that playing video games can improve motor coordination, visual recognition, spatial navigation, memory, reaction time, reasoning, decision-making, problem-solving skills, resilience, cooperation, and team participation. Playing video games can teach your brain new skills, which can be applicable not only in gaming but also in other aspects of life. Over 16 hours of gameplay, different types of games, such as 3-D adventure games, puzzle games, or rhythm gaming, can provide specific cognitive benefits. It is important to note that playing for long continuous periods is not recommended but incorporating a few hours of gameplay into your weekly leisure time can enhance neuroplasticity.

Learn a new language: Acquiring a new language offers significant cognitive benefits. Studies have shown that learning a new language can increase the density of gray matter in the brain, which is associated with language, attention, memory, emotions, and motor skills. Gray matter density can improve brain function, especially as you age, potentially protecting against cognitive decline. Learning a new language also strengthens white matter, which facilitates brain connectivity and communication between different brain regions. Benefits of language learning include stronger problem-solving and creative thinking skills, improved vocabulary, greater reading comprehension, and increased ability to multitask. Various resources like online programs, apps, textbooks, CDs, or local classified ads can help you start learning a new language.

Engage in music: Music has several benefits for the brain, including improving mood, learning and memory abilities, concentration, and focus. Music therapy has been shown to slow down cognitive decline in older adults and promote neuroplasticity when combined with dance, art, gaming, and exercise. Learning to play music in childhood can protect against age-related cognitive decline and improve cognitive performance in older adulthood. Musicians often exhibit better audio and visual perception, greater focus and attention, better memory, and better motor coordination. Learning to play an instrument or regularly listening to music can enhance brain neuroplasticity and provide these cognitive benefits.

Travel: Exploring new places and experiencing different scenery can enhance cognitive flexibility, inspire creativity, and broaden your worldview. It allows you to learn about diverse cultures and improve communication skills, contributing to cognitive benefits. If traveling widely is not currently possible, you can still take yourself on a "trip" closer to home by exploring new neighborhoods, trying different stores or restaurants, going for hikes, or virtually traveling through platforms like National Geographic on YouTube.

Exercise: Engaging in regular physical activity offers not only physical but also cognitive benefits. Aerobic exercise, in particular, can improve cognitive abilities such as learning, memory, fine motor coordination, and brain connectivity. Exercise promotes increased blood flow and cell growth in the brain, which is associated with reduced symptoms of depression. Exercising with others can provide social benefits, improving the quality of life and emotional well-being. It is recommended to incorporate some form of physical activity into your daily routine.

Create art: Engaging in artistic activities such as drawing and painting can enhance creativity, improve cognitive abilities, and strengthen existing connections in the brain. Artistic pursuits provide a means to express emotions, gain insight into personal struggles, and see the world from unique perspectives. Even simple doodling can activate the brain's default mode network, promoting mental relaxation and neuroplasticity. Whether through tutorials, books, or personal exploration, anyone can engage in artistic activities and experience the associated brain benefits.

In summary, contrary to previous beliefs, it is possible to rewire the brain through neuroplasticity. By incorporating activities such as playing video games, learning a new language, engaging in music, traveling, exercising, and creating art, you can promote positive neuroplasticity, enhance cognitive function, and potentially protect against cognitive decline.

Evidence that the mind can heal

5 Studies that Suggest that the Brain Can Heal the Body

1. In a study published in the journal PLoS ONE in 2008, researchers found that participants who received a placebo treatment for pain experienced a reduction in pain-related brain activity. This suggested that the brain can influence pain perception and that the placebo effect may be a mechanism for the brain to promote healing.

2. A study published in the journal Psychosomatic Medicine in 2016. Found that patients with chronic low back pain who participated in a mindfulness-based stress reduction program experienced changes in brain activity that were associated with pain reduction and improvements in physical functioning.

3. In a study published in the Journal of Alternative and Complementary Medicine in 2017, researchers found that patients with irritable bowel syndrome who received cognitive-behavioral therapy experienced changes in brain structure and function that were associated with improvements in symptoms.

4. A study published in the Journal of Psychiatric Research in 2018 found that patients with depression who received transcranial magnetic stimulation experienced changes in brain activity that were associated with improvements in depressive symptoms.

5. A study published in the Journal of Alternative and Complementary Medicine in 2019 found that patients with chronic pain who received acupuncture experienced changes in brain activity that were associated with reductions in pain intensity and improvements in physical functioning.

These studies suggest that the brain can influence the body's healing processes, and that interventions that target the brain. This included mindfulness-based stress reduction, cognitive-behavioral therapy, transcranial magnetic stimulation, and acupuncture, which may be effective in promoting healing and reducing symptoms in various conditions.

5 Medical Examples of Mind/Body healing: Here are 5 examples of conditions where the brain has been suspected to play a role in healing the physical body:

1. **Placebo effect:** The placebo effect is a well-known phenomenon where patients may experience an improvement in symptoms after receiving a treatment that has no active ingredients. This effect is thought to be driven by the brain's belief that the treatment is effective. More studies have strongly suggested that the placebo effect can cause changes in brain activity that are associated with pain reduction and other improvements in symptoms.

2. **Spontaneous remission:** Spontaneous remission is a term used to describe cases where a disease or condition suddenly disappears without explanation or treatment. While the exact mechanisms behind spontaneous remission are not well understood, it is thought that the brain may play a role in some cases by activating the body's natural healing processes.

3. **Mind-body therapies:** Mind-body therapies such as meditation, yoga, and tai chi have been studied for their potential to promote healing in various conditions, including chronic pain, cardiovascular disease, and

autoimmune disorders. These therapies are thought to work by activating the brain's relaxation response, which in turn can promote healing and reduce symptoms.

4. **Placebo surgery:** In some cases, placebo surgery has been used in clinical trials to test the efficacy of surgical procedures. In these studies, patients may undergo a surgical procedure or a sham procedure that mimics surgery, and the outcomes are compared to determine if the surgical procedure is effective. In some cases, patients who receive the placebo surgery may experience improvements in symptoms, suggesting that the brain may be able to promote healing even in the absence of an actual surgical procedure.

5. **Hypnosis:** Hypnosis is a technique that is sometimes used to treat pain, anxiety, and other conditions. During hypnosis, the brain is thought to enter a state of heightened suggestibility, which can allow the patient to introduce changes to their thoughts, feelings, and behaviors that can promote healing and reduce symptoms. While the exact mechanisms behind hypnosis are not well understood, studies have indicated that it can cause changes in brain activity that are associated with pain reduction and other improvements in symptoms.

There are documented medical cases where doctors have believed that the mind played a role in curing a physical ailment. Here are three examples:

1. **Spontaneous remission of cancer:** There have been cases where cancer patients have experienced spontaneous remission, where the cancer disappears without explanation or treatment. In some cases, doctors have attributed these remissions to the patient's mental state, such as their positive attitude or strong belief in their ability to fight cancer. One famous example is the case of Anita

Moorjani, who was diagnosed with stage 4 lymphoma and experienced a spontaneous remission after having a near-death experience, which she believes was due to a shift in her mindset and beliefs.

2. **Parkinson's disease:** In a study published in 2015 in the journal Neurology, researchers followed a group of patients with Parkinson's disease who underwent a placebo surgery where electrodes were implanted in their brains but not turned on. Interestingly, some patients experienced improvements in their symptoms despite not receiving any active treatment. The researchers believe that the placebo effect, driven by the patients' belief that they had received an effective treatment, may have played a role in the improvements.

3. **Irritable bowel syndrome:** In a study published in 2018 in the journal The Lancet Gastroenterology & Hepatology, researchers studied a group of patients with irritable bowel syndrome (IBS) who underwent a type of cognitive behavioral therapy called gut-directed hypnotherapy. The therapy involved teaching the patients techniques to reduce their stress and anxiety levels and to reframe their thoughts about their symptoms. The researchers found that the therapy was effective in improving the patients' symptoms, and they believe that the therapy worked by changing the patients' brain-gut interactions.

Pets and Positive Thoughts

Pets have a remarkable ability to bring joy, companionship, and love into our lives. They can also have a profound impact on our mental well-being and help us think positive thoughts. Here's a detailed explanation of how pets can contribute to positive thinking:

Unconditional Love and Acceptance: Pets offer unconditional love and acceptance. They don't judge us based on our flaws or mistakes. Their affectionate and non-judgmental nature creates a safe space where we can feel accepted and valued. Knowing that we are loved by our pets can boost our self-esteem, promote a positive self-image, and encourage positive thinking.

Emotional Support: Pets are excellent sources of emotional support. When we're feeling down, stressed, or anxious, their presence can provide comfort and solace. The act of petting or cuddling with a pet releases oxytocin, a hormone that promotes feelings of happiness and relaxation. This physical contact and emotional connection can help us shift our focus from negative thoughts to positive feelings of warmth and contentment.

Reduced Stress and Anxiety: Interacting with pets has been shown to reduce stress and anxiety levels. Spending time with a pet can lower cortisol (the stress hormone) and increase the production of endorphins (the feel-good hormones). These physiological changes can help alleviate negative emotions and promote a sense of calm and well-being. With reduced stress, our minds are more likely to be open to positive thoughts and perspectives.

Mindfulness and Living in the Present Moment: Pets have a natural ability to live in the present moment. When we engage with them, whether through play or simply observing their behavior, we are reminded to be present and fully engaged in the experience. This practice of mindfulness can help shift our focus away from negative thoughts associated with the past or future and bring us into the positive present moment.

Increased Social Connection: Owning a pet often leads to increased social interaction and connection with others. Whether we're taking our dog for a walk or engaging in activities related to our pet's care, we may encounter other pet owners or animal lovers. These social interactions can foster a sense of belonging, reduce feelings of loneliness, and provide opportunities for positive conversations and shared experiences.

Physical Activity and Well-being: Pets, particularly dogs, encourage physical activity. Regular exercise with a pet, such as walking or playing, promotes the release of endorphins, improves cardiovascular health, and increases overall well-being. Engaging in physical activity can help clear the mind, reduce stress, and create a positive mindset.

Responsibility and Purpose: Taking care of a pet instills a sense of responsibility and purpose in our lives. Knowing that another living being depends on us for their well-being can give us a sense of fulfillment and a positive sense of purpose. Caring for a pet can also provide a daily routine, structure, and a sense of accomplishment, which can contribute to positive thinking and mental well-being.

Laughter and Playfulness: Pets have a way of bringing laughter and playfulness into our lives. Their antics, playful behavior, and curiosity can be contagious and uplift our spirits. Laughter releases endorphins, reduces stress, and boosts our mood. By engaging in play and finding joy in our pets' presence, we can shift our focus to positive experiences and thoughts.

In summary, pets have a multitude of ways in which they contribute to positive thinking. Their unconditional love, emotional support, ability to reduce stress, promote mindfulness, increase social connection, and encourage physical activity and playfulness all contribute to a more positive mindset. By sharing our lives with pets, we can experience the profound benefits of their companionship, leading to increased happiness, optimism, and positive thoughts.

CHAPTER

4

Applying Positive Thinking

10 Examples of How Positive Thinking Can Help When Life is Not Going Well

Shifting Perspective: Positive thinking allows you to shift your perspective when facing difficult situations. Instead of getting stuck in a negative or defeatist mindset, positive thinking helps you view challenges as opportunities for growth and learning. By reframing problems as temporary obstacles rather than insurmountable barriers, you open your mind to creative problem-solving and resourceful thinking.

When you approach life's challenges with a positive mindset, you can view them as opportunities to develop resilience, learn new skills, and discover alternative paths to success. This shift in perspective broadens your problem-solving capabilities and enables you to explore different angles and solutions.

Cultivating Resilience: Positive thinking strengthens your resilience, allowing you to bounce back from setbacks and adapt to changing circumstances. When life is not going well, maintaining a positive outlook can help you weather the storm and persevere in the face of adversity. Positive thinking enables you to acknowledge and process negative emotions, but also empowers you to focus on solutions and possibilities.

By cultivating resilience through positive thinking, you develop the mental and emotional fortitude to tackle challenges head-on. You approach problems with a sense of determination and a belief in your ability to overcome obstacles. This resilience enables you to persist in problem-solving, even when faced with setbacks or failures along the way.

Encouraging Open-Mindedness: Positive thinking fosters open-mindedness, which is essential for effective problem-solving. When faced with difficult situations, negative thoughts and emotions can cloud your judgment and limit your ability to consider alternative perspectives or solutions. However, by adopting a positive mindset, you create space for fresh ideas and innovative approaches to problem-solving.

Positive thinking encourages you to explore different viewpoints, seek advice from others, and consider unconventional solutions. It opens your mind to possibilities that may have otherwise been overlooked. By embracing open-mindedness, you tap into your creativity and expand your problem-solving repertoire.

Strengthening Analytical Thinking: Positive thinking enhances analytical thinking, which is crucial for problem-solving. When life is not going well, it's easy to get caught up in negative emotions and react impulsively. However, positive thinking helps you step back, assess the situation objectively, and approach problems with a clear and logical mindset.

By maintaining a positive outlook, you can focus on the facts and data at hand, identify patterns or trends, and evaluate potential solutions based on their feasibility and effectiveness. This analytical thinking allows you to make informed decisions and choose the most appropriate course of action.

Boosting Creativity: Positive thinking fuels creativity, which is a valuable asset when facing challenging situations. When life throws you curveballs, a positive mindset encourages you to tap into your creative reserves and generate innovative solutions. Positive thinking sparks inspiration and encourages you to embrace innovative approaches.

By embracing positive thinking, you can engage in brainstorming, mind mapping, or other creative problem-solving techniques. This allows you to explore unconventional ideas, challenge assumptions, and discover novel approaches to solving concerns. Creativity, coupled with positive thinking, empowers you to find unique and effective solutions to life's challenges.

Fostering Adaptability: Positive thinking fosters adaptability, which is crucial when life is not going well. Problems and obstacles often require flexibility and the ability to adapt to new circumstances. Positive thinking helps you embrace change and approach difficulties with a mindset of flexibility and adaptability.

When faced with setbacks or unexpected circumstances, positive thinking allows you to remain open to new strategies or alternative paths. It helps you let go of rigid expectations and embrace a more fluid approach to problem-solving. This adaptability empowers you to adjust your plans and actions as needed, increasing your chances of finding effective solutions.

Building Confidence: Positive thinking builds confidence, which is essential for problem-solving. When life is challenging, it's common to doubt your abilities and feel overwhelmed. However, positive thinking helps you cultivate self-belief and trust in your problem-solving skills.

By focusing on your strengths and past successes, positive thinking reinforces your confidence in your ability to tackle issues and find solutions. This confidence fuels your motivation and determination, allowing you to approach challenges with a sense of self-assurance and resilience.

Enhancing Decision-Making: Positive thinking enhances your decision-making abilities, even when life is not going well. Negative emotions and thoughts can cloud your judgment and hinder effective decision-making. However, by maintaining a positive mindset, you can approach decisions with clarity and objectivity.

Positive thinking helps you maintain a balanced perspective, consider the pros and cons of different options, and make decisions based on rational thinking rather than impulsive reactions. It enables you to weigh the potential outcomes and choose the course of action that aligns with your goals and values.

Encouraging Persistence: Positive thinking encourages persistence in problem-solving. When faced with significant challenges, it's easy to feel discouraged and give up. However, positive thinking helps you maintain a sense of optimism and a belief in your ability to find solutions.

By adopting a positive mindset, you cultivate perseverance and determination. You view setbacks as temporary obstacles and setbacks as learning opportunities. This resilience and persistence allow you to stay committed to finding solutions, even when the road is tough.

Promoting Well-Being: Ultimately, positive thinking promotes overall well-being, which is crucial when life is not going well. When you keep a positive mindset, you nurture your mental, emotional, and physical health. This, in turn, provides a solid foundation for effective problem-solving.

Positive thinking reduces stress, enhances emotional well-being, and improves cognitive function. It allows you to approach problems with a clear and focused mind, enabling you to generate creative solutions and make sound decisions. By prioritizing your well-being through positive thinking, you equip yourself with the necessary tools to navigate life's challenges and find meaningful solutions.

Remember, positive thinking alone may not solve all your problems, but it is a powerful mindset that enhances your problem-solving abilities and promotes a proactive approach to life's challenges. It is important to combine positive thinking with practical action, seeking support when needed, and developing a comprehensive problem-solving strategy.

Detailed examples of how thinking positively can help you better your life and reach your goals:

Increased Motivation: Positive thinking fuels motivation and inspires you to take action towards your goals. By focusing on positive outcomes and possibilities, you cultivate a sense of enthusiasm and determination. This increased motivation propels you forward, enabling you to overcome obstacles and stay committed to achieving your goals.

Enhanced Self-Confidence: Positive thinking boosts self-confidence, which is crucial for personal growth and goal attainment. When you have a positive mindset, you believe in your abilities and strengths. This self-confidence allows you to step out of your comfort zone, take risks, and tackle challenges with a greater sense of self-assurance, ultimately increasing your chances of success.

Improved Resilience: Positive thinking cultivates resilience, helping you bounce back from setbacks and persevere in the face of adversity. It enables you to view challenges as opportunities for growth and learning, rather than insurmountable obstacles. This resilience allows you to stay focused on your goals, adapt to changing circumstances, and maintain a positive outlook even during difficult times.

Overcoming Limiting Beliefs: Positive thinking helps you challenge and overcome limiting beliefs that may be holding you back. It encourages you to reframe negative thoughts and replace them with more empowering and constructive beliefs. By adopting a positive mindset, you create a mental environment that supports personal growth and opens doors to new possibilities, allowing you to reach your goals with greater ease.

Improved Problem-Solving Skills: Positive thinking stimulates creative thinking and enhances problem-solving skills. When faced with challenges or roadblocks, a positive mindset enables you to approach them with a solution-oriented attitude. By focusing on positive outcomes and possibilities, you can generate innovative ideas, explore alternative approaches, and find effective solutions to overcome obstacles on your path to reaching your goals.

Building Strong Relationships: Positive thinking plays a vital role in building and maintaining strong relationships. When you approach interactions with positivity, you attract like-minded individuals and foster meaningful connections. Positive thinking enables you to communicate effectively, inspire others, and collaborate with others towards shared goals. Strong relationships provide support, encouragement, and opportunities, all of which contribute to your personal and professional growth.

Improved Mental and Emotional Well-being: Positive thinking has a significant impact on your mental and emotional well-being. It reduces stress levels, improves mood, and promotes a greater sense of overall happiness. When you maintain a positive mindset, you cultivate a more balanced perspective, effectively manage negative emotions, and experience greater overall well-being. This positive mental and emotional state allows you to focus on your goals and make progress towards achieving them.

Increased Productivity and Focus: Positive thinking enhances productivity and focus, leading to greater efficiency in working towards your goals. When you maintain a positive mindset, you have a clearer vision of your objectives, and you can prioritize tasks effectively. Positive thinking reduces distractions, boosts concentration, and helps you stay motivated and on track, allowing you to make consistent progress towards your goals.

Attracting Opportunities: Positive thinking creates a magnetic effect, attracting opportunities that align with your goals. When you radiate positivity, you become more open to recognizing and seizing opportunities as they arise. Positive thinking enables you to approach new experiences with a mindset of possibility and abundance, increasing the likelihood of encountering opportunities that can further your personal and professional growth.

Increased Life Satisfaction: Ultimately, positive thinking contributes to overall life satisfaction. When you cultivate a positive mindset and work towards your goals with optimism and determination, you create a life that aligns with your values and aspirations. Positive thinking allows you to appreciate and celebrate your achievements along the way, leading to a greater sense of fulfillment and contentment in life.

Remember, positive thinking should be accompanied by action, perseverance, and a realistic approach to goal-setting. It is a powerful tool that can shape your mindset and attitude, but it also requires effort and commitment to bring about meaningful change and achieve your goals.

10 Examples How Positive Thinking Can Help Your Mental State During an Illness

By focusing on positive thoughts and emotions, you can effectively reduce stress levels, promoting physical and mental relaxation. This, in turn, supports your immune system, improves sleep quality, and enhances your ability to cope with the demands of your illness.

Emotional Resilience: Cultivating emotional resilience is an essential aspect of positive thinking when dealing with an illness. It involves developing the ability to navigate the ups and downs of your illness journey with greater ease. Positive thinking helps you manage negative emotions such as fear, sadness, or anger, allowing you to maintain a more balanced and hopeful perspective. By consciously focusing on positive aspects and possibilities, you can regulate your emotions and find emotional strength. This emotional resilience empowers you to cope effectively with the emotional challenges of your illness, promoting overall mental well-being.

Enhancing Coping Strategies: Positive thinking enables you to develop and utilize effective coping strategies to deal with your illness. It encourages you to explore various techniques such as mindfulness, relaxation exercises, journaling, or seeking support from loved ones or support groups. By adopting a positive mindset, you become open to experimenting with different coping mechanisms that can help you manage pain, reduce stress, and improve your overall mental state. These coping strategies provide you with practical tools to navigate the emotional and physical aspects of your illness, contributing to your well-being.

Sense of Control: Positive thinking allows you to maintain a sense of control over your illness and its impact on your life. When facing an illness, it's common to experience feelings of helplessness or victimhood. However, by focusing on positive aspects and possibilities, you shift your attention away from those negative emotions. This positive mindset empowers you to take an active role in your healing journey. It helps you identify aspects within your control, such as adhering to treatment plans, making lifestyle changes, or seeking additional support. This sense of control enhances your self-efficacy and motivation to actively participate in your treatment, increasing your overall chances of improvement and well-being.

Building a Supportive Network: Positive thinking attracts a supportive network of family, friends, or healthcare professionals who can provide emotional and practical support during your illness journey. When you maintain a positive mindset, you radiate optimism and inspire others to be there for you. This positivity creates an environment where people are more inclined to offer understanding, encouragement, and a listening ear. Building a strong support network is crucial for your mental state when dealing with an illness. It provides you with a sense of connectedness, emotional support, and practical assistance, contributing to your overall well-being.

Finding Meaning and Purpose: Positive thinking helps you find meaning and purpose in your illness experience. While it may be challenging to find silver linings during difficult times, positive thinking allows you to reframe your perspective. By adopting a positive mindset, you can discover valuable life lessons, personal growth opportunities, and a deeper appreciation for the present moment. This search for meaning can bring a sense of fulfillment and contribute to your overall mental well-being as you navigate the challenges of your illness. It helps you maintain a sense of purpose and motivation, even in the face of adversity.

Improved Communication with Healthcare Providers: Positive thinking promotes effective communication with your healthcare providers. When you approach your medical appointments with a positive mindset, you are more likely to ask questions, seek clarification, and actively engage in shared decision-making. This open and positive communication fosters a stronger doctor-patient relationship, where you feel heard, understood, and actively involved in your treatment. When you maintain a positive attitude, you enhance your understanding of your illness and treatment options, which promotes a sense of empowerment and collaboration. This positive interaction with healthcare providers positively impacts your mental state, as you feel more confident and informed about your medical journey.

Resisting Negative Self-Talk: Positive thinking helps you resist negative self-talk and cultivates self-compassion. When dealing with an illness, it's common to experience self-blame, guilt, or feelings of inadequacy. However, positive thinking allows you to challenge those negative thoughts and replace them with self-affirming and supportive statements. By consciously focusing on positive aspects of yourself and your journey, you can cultivate self-compassion and nurture a healthier relationship with yourself. This self-compassion is crucial for your mental state, as it helps you maintain a positive self-image, promotes self-care, and reduces the impact of negative self-judgment on your well-being.

Enhancing Quality of Life: Ultimately, positive thinking can significantly enhance your overall quality of life while fighting an illness. By focusing on positive thoughts and emotions, you can maintain a higher level of psychological well-being. This positive mindset allows you to find moments of happiness, joy, and gratitude, even in the midst of your illness journey. It helps you make the most of each day, appreciating the present moment and cherishing the aspects of life that bring you joy. By nurturing a positive mental state, you can improve your overall quality of life, finding fulfillment and contentment during your challenges.

Remember, positive thinking should be complemented by proper medical treatment, professional support, and self-care practices. It is a powerful tool that can positively affect your mental state, but it is important to seek guidance from healthcare professionals and develop a comprehensive approach to your well-being during your illness.

5 Examples How Positive Thinking Can Help You Recover After Surgery

How positive thinking can help you after surgery and aid in your recovery:

Mind-Body Healing Connection: Positive thinking can establish a strong mind-body healing connection, which plays a significant role in the recovery process. By maintaining a positive mindset, you can enhance the production of endorphins and other positive neurotransmitters that contribute to pain management, stress reduction, and overall well-being. This positive outlook can positively impact your physical healing, allowing your body to respond more efficiently to treatment and recover more effectively.

Optimism and Resilience: Surgery and the recovery period can be physically and emotionally challenging. Positive thinking cultivates optimism and resilience, enabling you to face the recovery process with determination and hope. It helps you focus on the progress you make, no matter how small, and keeps you motivated to follow your post-operative instructions, adhere to medication schedules, and participate actively in your rehabilitation. This positive outlook promotes a more successful and smoother recovery.

Faster Rehabilitation Progress: Positive thinking can accelerate your rehabilitation progress after surgery. With a positive mindset, you are more likely to engage wholeheartedly in your physical therapy exercises, follow your healthcare provider's recommendations, and embrace lifestyle changes that support your recovery. The belief in your body's capacity to heal and regain strength can lead to better compliance with rehabilitation protocols, potentially resulting in faster healing and a quicker return to your normal activities.

Emotional Well-being and Stress Reduction: Surgery and recovery can often be accompanied by emotional distress and anxiety. Positive thinking helps in managing these emotions and reducing stress levels. By focusing on positive thoughts, practicing mindfulness techniques, and engaging in relaxation exercises, you can promote emotional well-being and create a calmer mental state. This, in turn, supports your physical recovery by reducing stress-related complications and aiding in pain management.

Building a Supportive Environment: A positive mindset can attract a supportive environment, which is crucial during the recovery period. When you approach your recovery journey with positivity, you radiate optimism and inspire those around you to supply the necessary support and encouragement. This can be from family, friends, healthcare professionals, or support groups. A positive and uplifting support system can offer emotional support, practical assistance, and motivation, all of which contribute to your overall recovery and well-being.

Remember, positive thinking should not replace medical advice or post-operative instructions. It is essential to consult your healthcare provider and follow their guidance throughout the recovery process. However, maintaining a positive mindset can significantly enhance your emotional well-being, physical healing, and overall experience during the recovery journey.

5 Examples How Positive Thinking Can Help You Out of an Emotional Rut

Five examples of how thinking positively can help you get out of an emotional rut:

Shifting Perspective: Positive thinking helps you shift your perspective and see things in a different light. When you're in an emotional rut, negative thoughts and emotions can dominate your mindset. Positive thinking allows you to challenge those negative thoughts and reframe the situation in a more positive and constructive way. This shift in perspective can help break the cycle of negativity and bring about a renewed sense of hope and optimism.

Self-Encouragement: Positive thinking involves practicing self-encouragement and self-compassion. When you're in an emotional rut, you may be prone to self-criticism and negative self-talk. Positive thinking allows you to counter those negative thoughts with self-affirming and empowering statements. By offering yourself kind and supportive words, you can boost your self-esteem, regain confidence, and break free from the emotional rut.

Gratitude Practice: Incorporating gratitude into your thinking can be a powerful tool to lift yourself out of an emotional rut. When you focus on the positive aspects of your life, even during challenging times, you cultivate a sense of appreciation and contentment. By practicing gratitude, whether through journaling or simply reflecting on what you're thankful for, you can shift your attention away from negative emotions and cultivate a more positive and hopeful mindset.

Engaging in Positive Activities: Positive thinking can prompt you to engage in activities that uplift your mood and bring you joy. When you're in an emotional rut, it can be challenging to find motivation or pleasure in anything. However, by consciously choosing to participate in activities that bring you happiness, such as hobbies, spending time with loved ones, or pursuing self-care practices, you can break the cycle of negativity and start to experience positive emotions again.

Seeking Support: Positive thinking encourages you to reach out for support when you're in an emotional rut. It's essential to share your feelings with trusted friends, family members, or a therapist who can provide a listening ear, empathy, and guidance. By seeking support, you allow yourself to be vulnerable and gain insights from others, which can help you gain a fresh perspective, find new coping strategies, and regain a sense of emotional balance.

Remember, thinking positively doesn't mean suppressing or ignoring negative emotions. It's about actively working to shift your mindset, nurture positive thoughts, and engage in behaviors that contribute to your well-being. If you find yourself constantly struggling with your emotions, it may be beneficial to seek professional help from a mental health professional, who can provide further guidance and support.

5 Examples How Positive Thinking Can Help You in Your Relationships

Positive thinking can positively impact your relationship:

Enhanced Communication: When you approach conversations and disagreements with a positive mindset, you create a safe and open space for effective communication. Positive thinking helps you avoid negative assumptions and jumping to conclusions, allowing you to actively listen to your partner's thoughts and feelings without judgment. This leads to better understanding, empathy, and the ability to find mutually beneficial solutions.

Resilience during Challenges: Every relationship faces its share of challenges, whether they are external factors or internal conflicts. Positive thinking helps you maintain a hopeful outlook, which in turn fosters resilience. Instead of getting overwhelmed by difficulties, you focus on finding solutions and adapting to the situation. You and your partner can face challenges as a team, knowing that you have the ability to overcome them and grow stronger together.

Increased Empathy: Positive thinking nurtures empathy within a relationship. It allows you to view your partner's actions and words in a more favorable light, assuming positive intentions rather than automatically assuming the worst. This mindset shift encourages you to put yourself in their shoes, trying to understand their perspective and emotions. By doing so, you build deeper connections and strengthen the bond between you.

Nurturing Appreciation: Positive thinking helps you cultivate a genuine appreciation for your partner and your relationship. It allows you to focus on their positive qualities, actions, and efforts, rather than fixating on their flaws or mistakes. Expressing appreciation through kind words, gestures, or acts of love creates a positive atmosphere in the relationship. Your partner feels valued and acknowledged, and this positivity fosters a deeper sense of connection and happiness.

Improved Emotional Well-being: Adopting positive thinking benefits the relationship and has a significant impact on your individual emotional well-being. When you consciously focus on the positive aspects of your partner and your relationship, you experience greater happiness, contentment, and fulfillment. Your positive mindset can also create a ripple effect, influencing your partner to adopt a more positive outlook as well. This positive feedback loop reinforces a healthy emotional state for both of you.

It's important to note that positive thinking should not be used to ignore or dismiss valid concerns or issues within the relationship. It should be coupled with open communication, active listening, and mutual effort from both partners to address and resolve any challenges. Ultimately, the power of positive thinking lies in its ability to foster a supportive and harmonious environment where love, understanding, and growth thrive.

5

Taking Action

Taking Positive Action When the Going Gets Tough

Fear is a natural human emotion designed to protect us from harm. But it can also hold us back from living to our fullest potential. When fear takes hold of your emotions, it's difficult to take action toward goals and dreams. However, there are ways to overcome fear's grip, build courage, and move forward.

The first step is recognizing when fear has hijacked your emotional state. Signs include anxiety, panic, paralysis, negative thinking, and avoidance. You may make excuses or procrastinate on meaningful endeavors. Take a pause to identify fear's presence. Tell yourself, "I'm feeling afraid, but this too shall pass." Name the fear to diffuse its power: "I'm afraid of failure/rejection/the unknown."

Once you've acknowledged the fear, reaffirm your capacity to handle challenges. Remind yourself of past successes in facing difficulties. We all have inner reservoirs of strength we can tap into, even if temporarily obscured by anxiety. Reflect on times you have been brave, strong, determined, resourceful and perseverant. You have these qualities even now. A current fearful emotion does not define you.

Label the emotions arising with curiosity and compassion. "Ah, there's anger arising with this fear, and also sadness." Anger usually masks more vulnerable feelings like hurt. Allow whatever may come up, without judgment. Emotions pass through us; they do not dictate who we are, unless we let them.

Regain internal balance and empowerment with centering practices, deep breathing, meditation, calming your mind. Breathe slowly in through your nose and out through your mouth. Feel the rise and fall of each inhalation and exhalation. Mentally scan your body and relax tension. Return to your anchor at the present moment.

Once you feel more centered, strategize how to move past the paralyzing effects of fear into constructive action. "What small step can I take now?" Break a big challenge down into smaller, bite-sized goals. Progress builds momentum and confidence. Stay focused on solutions.

Rather than refute fearful thoughts, practice reframing them. How else could you view the situation to see opportunities? What lessons could this difficulty present? Even setbacks hold valuable teachings if you shift perspective and trust in your ability to work through problems.

Surround yourself with positive influences. People, places, media - to elevate your mood and outlook. Limit time spent dwelling on anxious thoughts or with those encouraging fear. Nourish your spirit with inspiration and humor. Laughter helps lighten heavy moods.

Let your vision for the future guide you more than fear. Get clear on your goals, hopes, and dreams. Feel how actualizing them will serve you and others. Fears shrink when we stay focused on purposes larger than ourselves. Keep the big picture in mind.

Wherever attention goes, energy flows. Keep focused mentally on desired outcomes, solutions, strengths and next right actions, not on spiraling worries. Be present; fear is about imagined futures. Channel energy into creating rather than fretting.

Know that fear cannot actually stop you; only you can stop you. Feel the fear but choose to act anyway. Let fear move through and beyond you, rather than making decisions from that place of contraction. You still have choices.

Courage isn't the absence of fear, but the willingness to move through it. We build courageous "fear muscles" by exercising them, little by little. With consistent practice facing fears, we develop confidence in our ability to handle difficulties.

Reflect on how you want to look back on this time years from now. Will you regret letting fear hold you back? Or will you feel proud you took chances, learned and grew? What would the courageous, future you do now?

Trust in your capacity to figure out solutions as challenges arise. Perhaps the outcomes won't be perfect, but you'll grow wiser. Even temporary setbacks along the way serve to strengthen us. No effort toward growth is ever wasted.

Know there are resources within and around to assist you. Supportive people, inner strengths, spiritual forces bigger than us. You have more help available than you realize. Feel empowered, envisioning all the resources at your disposal now.

Staying stuck in inaction can generate more long-term stress than facing a difficulty would. We tend to overreact in our minds. Reality unfolds a step at a time; we handle as we go. Progress brings hope.

During challenging times, practice special self-care. Eat nourishing foods, rest well, move your body, seek beauty. Be kind and patient with yourself, aware of fear's tendency to trigger harsh self-criticism. Speak encouragingly to yourself.

Remember that fear cannot ultimately stop the unfolding of your purpose and highest potentials. Trust in your larger journey. Keep taking steps, however small, toward dreams. Let faith cast out fear.

I offer these reflections humbly, to inspire and remind us all that fear will not have the final word unless we let it. We can acknowledge its voice, yet still move forward with courage into growth, progress and purpose. This too shall pass. Onward.

Comparison between thinking positively and having negative or doubtful thoughts:

Thinking Positively:

Emotional Well-being: Thinking positively promotes emotional well-being. Positive thoughts and emotions, such as optimism, gratitude, and joy, have been linked to lower levels of stress, anxiety, and depression. When you think positively, you experience greater emotional resilience, allowing you to bounce back from setbacks and cope more effectively with challenges. Positive thinking fosters a sense of hope and optimism, which contributes to overall psychological well-being.

Problem-Solving Abilities: Positive thinking enhances problem-solving abilities. When you approach problems with a positive mindset, you are more likely to seek creative solutions, explore unconventional solutions, and persist in finding answers. Positive thinking broadens your perspective, allowing you to consider multiple possibilities and explore different approaches. It promotes a proactive approach to problem-solving, as you focus on finding solutions rather than dwelling on obstacles or limitations.

Resilience in the Face of Adversity: Positive thinking fosters resilience in the face of adversity. When confronted with challenges or setbacks, positive thinkers are more likely to view them as temporary and manageable. They maintain a belief in their ability to overcome obstacles, learn from failures, and grow stronger through adversity. Positive thinking enables individuals to reframe negative experiences as opportunities for personal growth, which contributes to their ability to bounce back and thrive in the face of adversity.

Improved Physical Health: Positive thinking has been associated with improved physical health outcomes. Studies have shown that individuals with positive attitudes have better cardiovascular health, stronger immune systems, and faster recovery rates from illness or surgery. Positive thinking promotes behaviors that contribute to physical well-being, such as engaging in regular exercise, maintaining a healthy diet, and seeking preventive healthcare. Moreover, positive thinkers are more likely to adhere to medical treatments and engage in self-care practices, leading to better overall health outcomes.

Enhanced Relationships: Positive thinking improves interpersonal relationships. When you approach relationships with a positive mindset, you are more likely to exhibit kindness, empathy, and forgiveness. Positive thinkers tend to have better communication skills, resolve conflicts more effectively, and build stronger connections with others. They create a positive and supportive environment that fosters trust, intimacy, and mutual understanding. Positive thinking also enhances your self-image and self-confidence, which positively impacts your relationships with others.

Having Negative or Doubtful Thoughts:

Increased Stress and Anxiety: Negative or doubtful thoughts contribute to increased stress and anxiety levels. When you constantly focus on negative outcomes or doubt your abilities, you create a cycle of worry and fear. These negative thoughts trigger the body's stress response, leading to heightened levels of cortisol and adrenaline. Prolonged exposure to stress and anxiety can have detrimental effects on both physical and mental health, including increased risk of cardiovascular diseases, weakened immune system, and decreased cognitive function.

Impaired Decision-Making: Negative or doubtful thoughts can impair decision-making abilities. When you constantly doubt yourself or expect negative outcomes, you may become paralyzed by indecision or make choices based on fear rather than rational thinking. Negative thoughts can cloud judgment, leading to poor decision-making and missed opportunities for growth or success. The constant self-doubt and negativity hinder your ability to consider alternative perspectives, evaluate options objectively, and choose the most appropriate course of action.

Limited Problem-Solving Strategies: Negative or doubtful thoughts limit your problem-solving strategies. When you approach problems with a negative mindset, you may focus on the limitations and barriers rather than exploring potential solutions. Negative thoughts can lead to a narrow perspective and hinder creativity, preventing you from considering alternative approaches or thinking outside the box. The lack of belief in your abilities and constant self-criticism can undermine your confidence and motivation to find effective solutions.

Negative Impact on Relationships: Negative or doubtful thoughts can negatively impact relationships. When you constantly doubt others' intentions or have a negative outlook on interactions, it can create a hostile or mistrustful environment. Negative thoughts can lead to misunderstandings, conflicts, and strained relationships. Moreover, constant self-doubt or negative self-talk can affect your self-esteem and confidence, which can hinder your ability to build and maintain healthy relationships.

Weakened Resilience: Negative or doubtful thoughts weaken resilience. When you consistently focus on negative outcomes or doubt your ability to overcome challenges, it becomes difficult to bounce back from setbacks. Negative thoughts perpetuate a sense of helplessness and victimhood, preventing you from taking proactive steps to overcome obstacles. This lack of resilience can lead to a cycle of negative thinking, as each setback reinforces the belief that success is unattainable.

In summary, thinking positively has numerous benefits for mental and physical well-being, problem-solving abilities, resilience, and relationships. Positive thinking promotes emotional well-being, enhances problem-solving skills, fosters resilience in the face of adversity, improves physical health, and strengthens relationships. On the other hand, negative or doubtful thoughts contribute to increased stress and anxiety, impair decision-making abilities, limit problem-solving strategies, negatively impact relationships, and weaken resilience. It is important to cultivate positive thinking patterns through self-awareness, practicing gratitude, challenging negative thoughts, and seeking support when needed.

You Can Kill the Pain

Yes, the brain can modulate or control the perception of pain, and this phenomenon is known as pain modulation or pain inhibition. The brain can release natural pain-relieving chemicals called endorphins and activate descending pathways that suppress pain signals. This can result in a reduction in the intensity of pain or even temporarily blocking pain signals altogether.

Scientific studies that demonstrate a connection between positive thinking and pain management

- A 2012 study published in the Journal of Pain Research found that participants who wrote positive thoughts about living with pain experienced a 20% decrease in pain intensity compared to those who wrote factual or negative statements.

- A 2014 systematic review published in the Annals of Behavioral Medicine analyzed 22 studies on positive psychology interventions for pain. It concluded that techniques like expressing gratitude, positive reframing of pain, and focusing on meaning helped reduce pain and improve well-being.

- A 2016 study in the journal PeerJ tested an intervention called Positive Cognitive Behavioral Therapy (P-CBT) for chronic pain patients. The P-CBT group reported significantly lower pain intensity and physical disability compared to standard CBT and treatment-as-usual control groups.

- A 2018 randomized controlled trial published in Annals of Behavioral Medicine found that optimistic thinking could increase pain tolerance and threshold. Participants who underwent an optimism boosting intervention were able to keep their hands in ice water for longer periods of time compared to controls.

- A meta-analysis in the journal Emotion reviewed 38 studies on emotion regulation and pain. It found that reappraisal strategies, including positively reinterpreting pain sensations, were effective in decreasing self-reported pain levels.

So, in summary, multiple rigorous studies and reviews have demonstrated that techniques aimed at fostering positive thinking, optimism, meaning, and emotional regulation can reduce self-reported pain intensity and increase pain tolerance. The evidence supports positive thinking as an evidence-based pain management approach.

Here are a few ways in which the brain can modulate pain:

Distraction: Engaging in activities or focusing on something else can divert attention away from the pain, which can lead to a perceived reduction in pain intensity.

Placebo effect: Believing that a treatment or intervention will relieve pain can activate the brain's natural pain-relieving mechanisms. Placebo responses involve the release of endorphins and other neurotransmitters that dampen pain signals.

Meditation and relaxation techniques: Practices such as meditation, deep breathing, and progressive muscle relaxation can help calm the mind and activate relaxation responses in the body. These techniques can trigger pain-inhibitory pathways in the brain.

Psychological and emotional factors: Emotions, mood, and mental states can influence pain perception. Positive emotions, such as happiness or excitement, can produce an analgesic effect, while negative emotions, stress, or anxiety can amplify pain perception.

Pharmacological interventions: Certain medications, such as opioids, can directly target the brain's pain pathways and modulate pain perception. These medications act on opioid receptors in the brain and spinal cord, blocking or reducing pain signals.

It's important to note that while pain modulation techniques can provide temporary relief or reduce the perception of pain, they do not address the underlying cause of the pain. It's essential to seek medical attention for proper diagnosis and treatment of any injury or condition causing pain.

The Mind/Body Neuro Connection: Can the Mind Actually Heal the Body?

The brain communicates with muscles through a complex network of neural pathways known as the motor system. This system involves multiple regions of the brain, including the primary motor cortex, premotor cortex, supplementary motor area, basal ganglia, cerebellum, and brainstem.

When you decide to move a specific muscle or perform a certain action, the motor cortex in the brain initiates the process. The motor cortex sends signals, in the form of electrical impulses, down the spinal cord through a bundle of nerve fibers called the corticospinal tract. These signals travel to the motor neurons in the spinal cord, which directly innervate the muscles.

The motor neurons act as intermediaries between the brain and the muscles. They receive signals from the motor cortex and transmit them to the muscles, causing muscle contraction. The motor neurons form synapses, or connections, with muscle fibers at specialized structures called neuromuscular junctions. When the signals from the motor neurons reach the neuromuscular junctions, they trigger the release of chemicals called neurotransmitters, such as acetylcholine, which stimulate the muscle fibers to contract.

The process of movement control also involves feedback loops. Sensory receptors located in the muscles, tendons, and joints provide information about the position, movement, and tension of the body. This sensory information is transmitted back to the brain through sensory pathways. The brain then uses this feedback to adjust and refine the motor commands, allowing for precise and coordinated movements.

The motor system is a highly intricate and coordinated network, involving various brain regions, neural pathways, and muscle interactions. It allows the brain to communicate with muscles and execute voluntary movements, ensuring our ability to interact with the environment.

The motor system and its pathways play a crucial role in helping people with physical ailments by enabling movement, mobility, and rehabilitation. Here are a few examples of how this system can be utilized in the context of physical ailments:

Physical therapy and rehabilitation: When individuals experience physical injuries, such as fractures, muscle strains, or joint dislocations, the motor system is involved in the recovery process. Physical therapists work with patients to design targeted exercises and activities that stimulate the motor pathways and promote healing. Through repetitive movements and specific exercises, the motor system is engaged, allowing for the reestablishment of muscle strength, coordination, and range of motion.

Neurological conditions: In cases of neurological conditions such as stroke, spinal cord injury, or multiple sclerosis, the motor pathways may be affected. Rehabilitation strategies, such as constraint-induced movement therapy or functional electrical stimulation, aim to activate the remaining neural pathways and promote neuroplasticity. These approaches can help individuals regain or improve motor function and regain independence in daily activities.

Prosthetics and assistive devices: In situations where individuals have lost limbs or have limited mobility, the motor system can be utilized with prosthetic limbs or assistive devices. Advanced prosthetics can be controlled using neural signals from the remaining muscles or even directly from the brain through techniques like brain-computer interfaces (BCIs). By interpreting the individual's intention to move, these technologies enable individuals to control and interact with their environment.

Parkinson's disease and movement disorders: Conditions such as Parkinson's disease, which involve disruptions in the motor system due to the degeneration of certain brain regions, can be managed through medication, deep brain stimulation, or other interventions. Deep brain stimulation involves implanting electrodes into specific brain regions to modulate abnormal electrical activity and improve motor symptoms.

In all these cases, understanding and utilizing the motor system's pathways are crucial for designing effective interventions and treatments. By targeting the damaged or affected areas and engaging the remaining neural connections, it becomes possible to enhance motor function, improve quality of life, and facilitate recovery for individuals with physical ailments.

The mind-body connection refers to the intricate relationship between our thoughts, emotions, beliefs, and our physical health and well-being. It recognizes that our mental and emotional state can significantly influence our physical health, and vice versa. Understanding and nurturing this connection can have a profound impact on our overall well-being. Here is a detailed explanation of the mind-body connection and some techniques to strengthen this connection:

Awareness and Mindfulness: One of the foundational techniques for strengthening the mind-body connection is developing awareness and practicing mindfulness. This involves intentionally bringing attention to the present moment, observing thoughts, emotions, and bodily sensations without judgment. By cultivating this awareness, we become more attuned to the signals our body sends us, such as physical tension, discomfort, or emotional stress. This heightened awareness allows us to respond to these signals in a more compassionate and proactive manner.

Deep Breathing and Relaxation Techniques: Deep breathing exercises and relaxation techniques help activate the body's relaxation response, which counteracts the effects of stress on our physical health. By consciously slowing down and deepening our breath, we engage the parasympathetic nervous system, promoting relaxation, reducing heart rate, and calming the mind. Practices like progressive muscle relaxation, guided imagery, or body scan meditation can also help release tension, promote a sense of calm, and enhance the mind-body connection.

Visualization and Guided Imagery: Visualization techniques involve using the power of imagination to create mental images that promote healing and well-being. Guided imagery sessions or self-guided visualization exercises can be used to envision positive outcomes, imagine the body healing, or visualize oneself in a state of optimal health. By engaging the senses and vividly imagining positive scenarios, we tap into the mind's ability to influence physical and emotional states.

Positive Affirmations and Self-Talk: The language we use internally and externally has a significant impact on our thoughts, emotions, and ultimately, our physical well-being. Positive affirmations involve consciously choosing and repeating positive statements about ourselves and our health. By affirming positive beliefs and reinforcing self-empowering thoughts, we can rewire our subconscious mind and shape our perception of our body's healing abilities.

Exercise and Movement: Physical activity is not only beneficial for our physical health but also plays a crucial role in the mind-body connection. Engaging in regular exercise releases endorphins, which are natural mood boosters, and reduces stress levels. Physical movement, whether through yoga, dancing, walking, or any other form of exercise, helps channel and release emotions, promotes a sense of well-being, and enhances the connection between mind and body.

Emotional Expression and Journaling: Emotions are an integral part of the mind-body connection. Suppressed or unexpressed emotions can manifest as physical symptoms or ailments. Engaging in emotional expression through journaling, talking to a trusted friend or therapist, or engaging in creative outlets can help release emotional blockages and promote healing. Writing down thoughts and emotions in a journal provides an opportunity for reflection, gaining insight, and making connections between emotional states and physical well-being.

Mind-Body Practices: There are various mind-body practices that specifically target the mind-body connection. These include practices such as yoga, tai chi, qigong, and mindfulness-based stress reduction (MBSR). These practices combine physical movement, breath-work, mindfulness, and relaxation techniques to promote a harmonious connection between the mind and body. Regular practice of these techniques helps cultivate a deep sense of awareness, balance, and overall well-being.

It's important to note that everyone's experience with the mind-body connection may vary, and it is a personal journey of exploration and self-discovery. These techniques provide a starting point for nurturing and strengthening the mind-body connection, but it's essential to find what works best for you and adapt them to your unique needs and preferences. Consistent practice and an open mindset can help deepen your understanding of the mind-body connection and unlock its transformative potential for your overall health and well-being.

Communication between the mind and body

Scientists have conducted extensive research on the mind-body connection and have uncovered fascinating findings regarding the power of the mind to influence physical healing. Here is a detailed summary of what scientists have discovered:

Placebo Effect: The placebo effect is a well-documented phenomenon where a patient experiences improvements in their health after receiving a treatment with no active therapeutic ingredients. The belief and expectation of receiving a beneficial treatment can trigger physiological changes in the body, such as pain relief or improved immune function. This demonstrates the significant role that the mind plays in the healing process.

Mind-Body Techniques: Various mind-body techniques, such as meditation, visualization, and relaxation exercises, have been shown to impact physical health positively. These practices elicit the relaxation response, which counteracts the effects of stress and promotes healing. Studies have demonstrated that mind-body techniques can reduce pain, enhance immune function, regulate blood pressure, and improve overall well-being.

Neuroplasticity: Neuroplasticity refers to the brain's ability to reorganize itself and form new neural connections throughout life. Research has shown that positive thoughts, emotions, and beliefs can stimulate neuroplasticity and promote healing. By consciously cultivating positive thinking patterns, individuals can reshape their brain circuits, leading to improved health outcomes.

Stress Reduction: Chronic stress has a profound impact on physical health and can increase the risk of various diseases. Studies have shown that stress reduction techniques, such as mindfulness-based stress reduction (MBSR) or relaxation exercises, can positively influence the body's stress response. By managing stress, individuals can enhance immune function, reduce inflammation, and improve their overall health and healing capacity.

Mind-Body Communication: The mind and body are intricately connected through a complex network of communication pathways. Research has demonstrated that thoughts and emotions can influence physiological processes, including heart rate, blood pressure, hormone production, and immune function. Positive thoughts and emotions have been associated with enhanced immune response, improved wound healing, and faster recovery from surgeries or injuries.

Mindfulness-Based Interventions: Mindfulness-based interventions, such as Mindfulness-Based Stress Reduction (MBSR) and Mindfulness-Based Cognitive Therapy (MBCT), have gained attention for their positive effects on physical health. These interventions involve training individuals to cultivate non-judgmental awareness of the present moment, which can reduce stress, enhance emotional well-being, and improve physical health outcomes.

The Role of Beliefs and Expectations: Beliefs and expectations can shape our perception of health and influence our healing process. Studies have shown that individuals with positive beliefs and optimistic outlooks tend to experience better health outcomes, including reduced pain, improved recovery, and increased overall well-being. Believing in the body's innate capacity to heal and having confidence in medical treatments can have a profound impact on the healing process.

Overall, scientific research has consistently demonstrated the powerful connection between the mind and the body in influencing physical healing. By harnessing the power of the mind through various positive thought techniques and practices, individuals can play an active role in their own healing journey and optimize their overall well-being.

Techniques for a Positive Mind

The Mind and Our Potential

The power of the mind is a fascinating and multifaceted aspect of human potential. It plays a crucial role in driving us toward great achievements. Here's a detailed exploration of how the power of the mind can stimulate us to reach extraordinary heights:

Motivation and Goal Setting: The mind can create and sustain motivation, which is essential for achieving great things. By setting clear goals and visualizing success, the mind can ignite a sense of purpose and drive that propels us forward. It helps us focus our attention, prioritize tasks, and overcome obstacles along the way.

Positive Mindset and Self-Belief: A positive mindset is a powerful tool that allows us to overcome self-doubt, fear, and adversity. The mind can shape our beliefs and perceptions, which in turn influence our actions and outcomes. When we cultivate a belief in our abilities, resilience, and optimism, we are more likely to take risks, persevere through challenges, and ultimately achieve our goals.

Visualization and Mental Imagery: The mind has the remarkable ability to create mental images and scenarios that can positively impact our performance. Through visualization, we can vividly imagine ourselves successfully completing tasks, achieving goals, and overcoming obstacles. This mental rehearsal enhances our confidence, focus, and neural connections related to the desired skills, thereby improving our actual performance.

Concentration and Flow States: The power of the mind lies in its capacity to focus and concentrate. When we engage in deep concentration, we enter a state of flow—a state of complete immersion and optimal performance. In this state, distractions fade away, and our mind operates in a highly efficient and productive manner. The ability to harness this mental state can lead to incredible achievements and peak performance.

Emotional Regulation and Resilience: The mind can regulate our emotions, allowing us to remain resilient in the face of setbacks, failures, and difficulties. By cultivating emotional intelligence, we can manage stress, stay focused, and bounce back from challenges. The power of the mind lies in its ability to reframe negative experiences, learn from them, and use them as stepping stones toward greater achievement.

Creativity and Innovation: The mind is a wellspring of creativity and innovation. By exploring new ideas, making connections between seemingly unrelated concepts, and exploring unconventional solutions, we can unlock breakthroughs and achieve remarkable feats. The power of the mind lies in its capacity to imagine possibilities, challenge conventional thinking, and pave the way for transformative achievements.

Mind-body Connection: The mind and body are intricately linked, and the power of the mind extends to physical achievements as well. By harnessing the mind-body connection, we can improve physical performance, endurance, and overall well-being. Techniques such as mindfulness, meditation, and visualization can enhance focus, reduce stress, and optimize physiological processes, leading to greater physical accomplishments.

In summary, the power of the mind is a potent force that can stimulate us to achieve great things. By harnessing motivation, maintaining a positive mindset, leveraging visualization, cultivating concentration, regulating emotions, fostering creativity, and embracing the mind-body connection, we can unlock our full potential and accomplish extraordinary feats.

99 Examples of What to Think and actions to take

1. Getting laid off from a job. Seeing it as an opportunity to find a new job better suited to your skills and interests. Take time to reflect on what you enjoyed and gain clarity on a better career path before jumping into applications.

2. Having a big argument with your spouse - Choosing to talk it out calmly and focus on resolving the issue constructively. Set egos aside, listen to understand each other's perspective, and find middle ground.

3. Struggling with a difficult class - Approaching it as a chance to develop grit and perseverance, which will help you later in life. Put in consistent effort, ask questions when stuck, and stay motivated by focusing on how mastering challenges expands your abilities.

4. Recovering from an injury or illness - Focusing on following doctor's orders so you can heal faster and get your strength back. Give your body what it needs through rest, proper nutrition, medications, and therapy so you can recover well.

5. Fighting an addiction - Believing that you can beat it and taking it one day at a time to stay clean and sober. Find support in others in recovery, avoid temptation triggers, and feel proud of every day you break the addiction cycle.

6. Being bullied - Refusing to let it get you down and instead standing up for yourself with courage. Don't internalize hurtful words, walk away from toxic people, and advocate for yourself by reporting bullying.

7. Failing an exam - Deciding to learn from your mistakes and come back stronger and better prepared next time. Review what tripped you up, improve your study habits going forward, and know you have the ability to succeed.

8. Losing a competition - Using it as motivation to train harder and give your absolute best effort moving forward. Analyze your performance, fine-tune your skills, and visualize winning next time.

9. Getting rejected from something you want - Persisting and trying again rather than giving up on your dream. Evaluate why you were rejected, strengthen your application, and keep chasing your goal.

10. Having a falling out with a close friend - Reaching out to reconnect and restore the friendship if possible. Be vulnerable, apologize for your role, and highlight how much the relationship means.

11. Being diagnosed with a serious illness - Focusing on your treatment plan and surrounding yourself with positive supporters. Educate yourself on your condition, follow your doctor's advice, and lean on loved ones for strength.

12. Going through a divorce - Choosing to have an amicable split and prioritizing your children's well-being. Compromise on conflicts, keep conversations respectful, and reassure kids they are loved.

13. Being in a car accident - Being grateful that you survived and no one was seriously injured. Focus on recovering physically and emotionally, repair damages responsibly, and cherish life's fragility.

14. Running up debt - Making a repayment plan to become debt-free over time through budgeting. Evaluate spending, reduce expenses, increase income, and make steady payments.

15. Getting passed over for a promotion - Deciding to expand your skills and try again in the future. Ask for candid feedback, obtain extra training, and demonstrate your readiness to try again.

16. Having low self-esteem - Working on developing confidence by focusing on your strengths. Make a list of positive qualities, challenge negative self-talk, and undertake things that make you feel accomplished.

17. Feeling lonely - Trying to meet new people and be friendly. Join groups for hobbies you enjoy, strike up conversations, and say yes to social invitations.

18. Losing a loved one - Honoring their memory by living your life fully. Share stories and pictures of them, carry on cherished traditions, and emulate their best qualities.

19. Moving to a new city - Embracing the adventure and opportunity to experience somewhere new. Explore the sights, try new activities, and put effort into meeting neighbors.

20. Going through a breakup - Allowing yourself to grieve, then looking ahead to new beginnings. Spend time with supportive friends, do things independently you enjoy, and know you will fall in love again.

21. Facing discrimination - Speaking out against it with the hope of inspiring change. Report incidents through proper channels, participate in anti-discrimination causes, spread compassion.

22. Developing a chronic health condition - Committing to manage it so you can live your best life. Learn all you can about your illness, follow your doctor's advice, and find your "new normal."

23. Pursuing a passion that others don't understand - Following your heart anyway. Focus on what fulfills you rather than impressing others, surround yourself with encouragers, and tune out naysayers.

24. Facing homelessness - Believing you can get back on your feet with perseverance. Connect with shelters and social

services, seek job and housing assistance, and don't lose hope for stability.

25. Coping with trauma - Getting help and allowing yourself to heal. Seek counseling to process painful memories, be gentle with yourself moving through grief, and trust you will feel joy again.

26. Messing up at your job - Learning from it and striving to do better next time. Take responsibility for the mistake, ask how you can improve, and implement lessons learned.

27. Feeling creatively blocked - Trying new approaches to get unstuck and spark fresh ideas. Shift gears completely, expose yourself to inspirational works, and revisit what first sparked your passion.

28. Declaring bankruptcy - Starting over financially wiser than before. Review what caused the bankruptcy, create a lean budget, rebuild credit slowly, and get educated on personal finance.

29. Wanting to start a business but lacking confidence - Taking a chance on yourself and going for it. Conduct market research, make a viable business plan, and take a leap of faith in your abilities.

30. Feeling disconnected from your culture - Trying to engage with it more authentically. Travel to your homeland if possible, participate in cultural events and causes, and befriend others who share your heritage.

31. Getting negative feedback - Taking constructive criticism humbly and investigating how to improve. Listen without defensiveness, ask clarifying questions, and implement suggested changes.

32. Dealing with infertility - Exploring different options for having a family. Seek medical help, consider alternatives

like adoption or surrogacy, and know your value is not defined by fertility.

33. Struggling as a single parent - Reaching out for help from friends and family. Share childcare duties, identify community resources like support groups, and don't be afraid to ask for what you need.

34. Moving for your spouse's job - Embracing the chance to discover a new place. Immerse yourself in your new community, try novel hobbies and activities, and intentionally build local friendships.

35. Taking care of elderly parents - Finding meaning in being able to give back to them. Cherish time spent together, express gratitude for all they did for you, and explore help options when required.

36. Feeling uninspired at your job - Revitalizing your passion for meaningful work. Focus on how your work positively impacts others, vary your routine, and make time for interests outside work.

37. Facing a moral dilemma - Following your principles to make the ethical choice. Listen to your conscience, evaluate all options, and have the courage to do what you'll feel proud of.

38. Preparing for an important exam - Believing in yourself and studying diligently. Visualize success, manage your time wisely, take practice tests, and know you can ace it.

39. Recovering from a natural disaster - Banding together with your community to rebuild. Provide and accept help from neighbors, focus on collective healing, and work cooperatively to restore normalcy.

40. Being nervous about asking someone out - Getting the courage to make your interest known. Calm your nerves,

remember the request can be flattering even if declined, and know it's a vulnerable risk worth taking.

41. Facing a legal dispute - Trusting the justice system and defending the truth. Seek good legal counsel, provide all documentation, and have faith that justice will prevail.

42. Battling an addiction - Taking it one day at a time and relying on your support system. Avoid triggers, lean on others in recovery and loved ones, and stay focused on your sobriety.

43. Coping with mental illness - Committing to your treatment plan and prioritizing self-care. Take medications as prescribed, attend therapy, eliminate unnecessary stress, and be patient with yourself.

44. Raising a strong-willed child - Fostering open communication and focusing on connection. Listen without judgment, find common ground, acknowledge their independence appropriately.

45. Going through menopause - Embracing this new phase of life with grace. Stay on top of treatment for symptoms, reconnect with your purpose, and relish gaining wisdom through life experiences.

46. Wanting to repair a damaged friendship - Reaching out humbly and asking for forgiveness. Take accountability for your mistakes, appeal to shared history, and be open to rebuilding trust slowly over time.

47. Getting laid off close to retirement - Seeing it as a chance to pursue long-held passions. Explore exciting new possibilities, take dream vacations, and embrace a less stressful pace of life.

48. Fighting systemic injustice - Believing progress is possible if people unite for good. Raise awareness respectfully, support leaders creating change, and set an example through your actions.

49. Caring for a sick pet - Focusing on providing comfort until the very end. Give medication properly, meet their needs gently, and show your love through affection.

50. Confronting fears - Taking small, courageous steps forward. Face manageable challenges, visualize positive outcomes, and replace worry with preparation.

51. Feeling disconnected from your partner - Scheduling intentional quality time to reconnect. Plan regular date nights, remove distractions during time together, and engage in open communication.

52. Realizing a dream isn't right for you anymore - Adjusting your life goals and finding a new path. Be honest with yourself about changing needs, get clarity on what matters now, and pivot your course decisively.

53. Getting criticism from your boss - Listening openly and striving to improve. Hear it as wanting you to succeed, ask for specific suggestions, and implement recommendations.

54. Dealing with problem neighbors - Extending good will and communicating respectfully. Make introductions, find common interests, and compromise on issues.

55. Coping with an empty nest - Discovering new purpose as your children grow independent. Reconnect with your partner, pursue neglected passions, and offer advice when asked as their mentor.

56. Recovering from an accident - Trusting that with time and care, healing is possible. Follow doctor recommendations diligently, celebrate small milestones, and visualize yourself restored.

57. Trying to get pregnant - Relying on your partner and doctor for support during the journey. Track cycles carefully, communicate openly about feelings, and trust medical expertise.

58. Wanting to change careers - Believing in your ability to gain new skills. Identify transferable strengths, pursue added training or education, and make yourself an attractive candidate.

59. Feeling disorganized and scattered - Making an achievable plan to provide direction. Break big goals into small steps, create systems to establish order, and progress one task at a time.

60. Going through a spiritual crisis - Allowing inner wisdom to guide your path. Listen to your heart in stillness, trust in a higher plan unfolding, and stay open to growth.

61. Confronting your privilege - Listening to marginalized voices with an open heart. Recognize unfair advantages with humility, support policies fostering equity, and become an ally.

62. Facing retirement - Embracing your next adventure filled with family, passions, and purpose. Plan for desired travel and hobbies, set meaningful goals, and celebrate entering this new season.

63. Taking an important exam - Visualizing success and thoroughly preparing. Commit to a study schedule, get plenty of rest, and imagine excelling with confidence.

64. Trying to heal an illness naturally - Having faith in the body's ability to restore balance. Eat nutritious foods, supplement wisely, support vitality through movement and mindfulness.

65. Pushing yourself physically - Focusing on progress, however small, and being proud. Celebrate fitness milestones, practice self-compassion on off days, and feel your strength growing.

66. Wanting to repair a damaged relationship - Approaching gently and appealing to shared history. Make thoughtful gestures, bring up the past fondly, and suggest making new positive memories.

67. Feeling like you don't belong - Believing your unique gifts are needed in this world. Identify communities that

appreciate your spirit, contribute your special talents, and quell self-doubt.

68. Going to couple's counseling - Giving it your all to reconnect and build greater intimacy. Have an open mind, do assigned practices, express yourself honestly, and trust the process.

69. Longing to start a family - Envisioning the day you become parents and believing it will come. Discuss options like IVF openly, focus on your strong relationship, and know life rarely goes as planned.

70. Volunteering your time - Knowing your contribution makes the world a little brighter. Find causes aligned with your passion, give wholeheartedly, and spread your spirit.

71. Moving for an exciting opportunity - Embracing a new community with openness. Make efforts to meet people, say yes to chances to connect, and become involved locally.

72. Making an important speech - Channeling nervousness into passion for your message. Thoroughly prepare your content, visualize connecting with your audience, and take deep breaths.

73. Confronting prejudice - Speaking out with courage, wisdom, justice, and love. Share your experience thoughtfully, appeal to common humanity, and model tolerance.

74. Recovering from injury or illness - Focusing completely on your self-care and healing. Heed medical advice, nourish your body with good foods and rest, and be extra gentle with yourself.

75. Facing major life changes - Viewing it as a journey of growth and self-discovery. Embrace the unknown as an adventure, reflect on lessons learned, and grow into your new role.

76. Longing for different political leadership - Believing your voice can contribute to needed change. Support candidates aligning with your vision, respectfully discuss issues with others, and trust in democracy.

77. Considering leaving an unfulfilling relationship - Envisioning life on your terms. Honestly assess your needs, imagine embracing new opportunities solo, and make an empowered choice.

78. Starting a new habit like exercising or meditating - Approaching kindly when you struggle. Focus on creating consistency, celebrate small successes, and grant yourself grace on difficult days.

79. Feeling uncertain about a risk - Weighing options while trusting your judgment. List pros and cons, seek wise counsel, examine your motivations, and have faith in your discernment.

80. Moving for your partner's job - Immersing yourself in a new community. Explore your surroundings with curiosity, join local groups, and regularly meet neighbors.

81. Wanting better work-life balance - Setting healthy boundaries and limiting distractions. Stick to defined work hours, set technology limits, and prioritize family and self-care.

82. Going to therapy - Giving it your all to gain insight and create positive change. Arrive open-minded, embrace discomfort, do homework exercises, and trust the power of awareness.

83. Dealing with a toxic family member - Setting loving limits while protecting your peace. Stand by your values, distance yourself when needed, and find good people to create your chosen family.

84. Confronting unhealthy patterns - Believing you can select new habits serving your growth. Get accountability and support, replace negative behaviors consciously, and celebrate each victory.

85. Co-parenting with an ex - Aiming for mutual respect and prioritizing the kids. Communicate effectively, allow each other time with children, and keep focused on their well-being.

86. Getting let go from a job - Seeing it as a chance to pursue work more aligned with your purpose. Reflect on your passions and skills, use severance for bills, and trust you will find something better.

87. Recovering from burnout - Making your health and self-care a top priority. Get plenty of rest, set controls around work, nourish yourself wholesomely, and make time for relaxation.

88. Longing for lost loved ones - Cherishing your memories while moving forward in hope. Revisit meaningful mementos and stories, recreate shared activities, and find comfort sensing their lasting presence.

89. Facing major surgery - Entrusting your care to skilled doctors and visualizing full recovery. Follow all pre-op directions thoroughly, have faith in the medical team, and see yourself becoming fully healthy.

90. Comforting a grieving friend - Listening with compassion and validating their pain. Provide shoulders to cry on, share memories of the deceased, assure them the anguish will lessen.

91. Going to family counseling - Humbly engaging for better understanding and harmony. Share your perspective honestly, listen without interrupting, and complete exercises assigned to facilitate bonding.

92. Dealing with scarcity of resources - Collaborating creatively with others to find solutions. Brainstorm possibilities, delegate tasks, contribute your abilities generously, and have hope.

93. Feeling discouraged about life - Reconnecting to your inner light and purpose. Meditate on what provides meaning, visualize rising above challenges, and help others.

94. Moving to an unfamiliar city - Embracing new adventures and friends. Introduce yourself to neighbors, accept invites, ask for recommendations, and know each day gets easier.

95. Pursuing your purpose despite challenges - Believing in your vision and abilities. Recall why your work matters, pray for strength and guidance, and trust your gifts will carry you through.

96. Preparing for a difficult conversation - Approaching with empathy, honesty, and care. Pray for wisdom, reflect on understanding all perspectives, and focus on resolving issues constructively.

97. Going on a long journey alone - Viewing it as an exciting opportunity for self-growth. Make plans flexible to discover hidden gems, journal your insights, and feel proud of independence.

98. Facing a setback toward your dreams - Persisting with resilience, faith and hard work. Lean on your support system, learn from failures, rest when needed, and know consistency pays off.

99. Any challenge life presents - Meeting it with courage, wisdom, hope!

25 Examples Where Negative Thoughts Can Be Harmful

1. Starting a new job - Thinking you don't have the skills or can't meet expectations. This undermines your confidence and prevents you from giving your best effort. Go in open-minded and trust your abilities.

2. Taking a test - Assuming you will fail because you did not study enough. This creates anxiety that disrupts recall and clear thinking during the test. Prepare your best and visualize success.

3. Asking someone on a date - Believing they will reject you, and you are not good enough. This stops you from putting yourself out there and finding potential happiness. Have confidence in your worthiness.

4. Learning a new skill - Thinking you lack talent and will never improve. This becomes a self-fulfilling prophecy. Focus on small wins and be patient with the process.

5. Recovering from illness - Doubting your body's healing capabilities. This weakens the immune system and motivation for healthy habits. Have faith in your inner strength.

6. Public speaking - Expecting poor performance because of nerves. This heightens anxiety to paralyzing levels. Channel nervous energy into passion for your message.

7. Competing in a sport - Assuming a more talented opponent will beat you. This resigns you to defeat instead of giving full effort. Remain focused only on your performance.

8. Making lifestyle changes - Being convinced old habits are impossible to break. This provides justification for giving up quickly. Know change takes time and commitment.

9. Saving money - Believing you will always overspend, making budgeting pointless. This becomes a self-fulfilling behavior. Build in accountability and rewards.

10. Repairing a relationship - Assuming your partner is unwilling to reconcile. This prevents communication and conflict resolution. Lead with openness and honesty.

11. Asking for a raise - Thinking your boss will say you do not deserve it. This stops you from asserting your value. Quantify your contributions and ask confidently.

12. Starting a business - Assuming it will just fail based on statistics. This negates all the hard work, passion, and skill you bring. Take the risk, believing in your vision.

13. Learning a second language - Convincing yourself you are too old, and it is too hard. This attitude hinders progress before you even start. Set small attainable goals and reward milestones.

14. Beginning an exercise program - Dwelling on how out of shape you are now. This tempts you to quit before even allowing your fitness to improve. Trust that your body will respond positively.

15. Cooking for guests - Worrying about mistakes or negative reviews. This distracts you, causing the very errors you wish to avoid. Focus on enjoying the process and company.

16. Expressing feelings in a relationship - Fearing rejection if your partner does not reciprocate. This leads to emotional bottling that breeds resentment. Have courage to respectfully share your heart.

17. Asking for support - Assuming friends and family are too busy to help. This deprives loved ones of the gift of supporting you. Give them a chance to show up for you.

18. Making choices - Second guessing every decision out of exaggerated fear of failure. This paralysis leaves you stuck. Evaluate options rationally, then act decisively.

19. Volunteering - Thinking you have nothing worthwhile to contribute. This keeps you on the sidelines instead of impacting lives for the better. Every person has something unique to give.

20. Traveling somewhere new - Believing you will dislike the food, culture, and people. This lens prevents you from embracing the experience. Approach with openness and curiosity.

21. Adopting a pet - Worrying you will be an inadequate owner. This anxiety interferes with bonding and providing proper care. Have confidence in your ability to love.

22. Performing or competing - Letting nerves convince you that you will forget everything you know. This often triggers the very memory blocks you wish to avoid. Stay present and trust your abilities.

23. Going on a first date - Assuming you will do something embarrassing or be boring. This self-consciousness makes you less relaxed and authentic. Have fun getting to know someone new!

24. Presenting creative work - Focusing on possible criticisms rather than the courage it took to share. This steals satisfaction and stunts budding talent. Own your worth and receive feedback humbly.

25. Applying for a new opportunity - Thinking, extensive experience and total confidence are required. This stops many worthy candidates from going for growth. Highlight your assets and take a chance!

50 Positive Things to Tell Yourself Over and Over

1. This too shall pass.

2. Tough times never last, but tough people do.

3. Every day may not be good, but there is something good in every day.

4. Turn your wounds into wisdom.

5. Don't give up. The beginning is always the hardest.

6. The pain you feel today is the strength you feel tomorrow.

7. Believe in yourself and all that you are.

8. Everything will be okay in the end. If it's not okay, it's not the end.

9. Hope sees the invisible, feels the intangible, and achieves the impossible.

10. Joy comes in the morning.

11. If opportunity doesn't knock, build a door.

12. When you change the way you look at things, the things you look at change.

13. Trust the wait. Embrace the uncertainty. Enjoy the beauty of becoming.

14. Keep going. Everything you need will come to you at the perfect time.

15. Smile and the world will smile back.

16. Stay strong, make them wonder how you're still smiling.

17. Rainbows follow the rain.

18. Success doesn't just find you. You have to go out and get it.

19. The struggle you're in today is developing the strength you require for tomorrow.

20. There is always, always, always something to be grateful for.

21. Whenever something bad happens, there is something good that you can take from it.

22. Take it day by day and be grateful for the little things.

23. Believe in your abilities, believe in yourself, and keep pushing forward.

24. Don't wait for an opportunity. Create it.

25. Be fearless in pursuit of what sets your soul on fire.

26. You are braver than you believe and stronger than you seem.

27. Worrying does not empty tomorrow of its troubles. It empties today of its strength.

28. Half of life is just showing up.

29. Your future is created by what you do today, not tomorrow.

30. The journey of a thousand miles begins with a single step.

31. Every champion was once a contender that refused to give up.

32. Believe you can and you're halfway there.

33. When you stop chasing the wrong things, you give the right things a chance to catch you.

34. Don't be pushed around by the fears in your mind. Be led by the dreams in your heart.

35. Happiness is not by chance, but by choice.

36. You'll never reach your destination if you stop to throw stones at every dog that barks.

37. Things turn out best for people who make the best out-of-the-way things turn out.

38. Courage doesn't always roar. Sometimes courage is the quiet voice at the end of the day saying 'I will try again tomorrow'.

39. You can if you think you can.

40. Character cannot be developed in ease and quiet. Only through experience of trial and suffering can the soul be strengthened.

41. Change the way you look at things, and the things you look at change.

42. We must embrace pain and burn it as fuel for our journey.

43. I am thankful for all those difficult people in my life, they have shown me exactly who I do not want to be.

44. Smile, breathe and go slowly.

45. Stay close to anything that makes you glad you are alive.

46. Inhale the future, exhale the past.

47. This is a new day. A new beginning. I am here. I am ready.

48. You're braver than you believe, stronger than you seem, and smarter than you think.

49. I have not failed. I've just found 10,000 ways that won't work.

50. Look for the rainbow in every storm.

When I was 25, I purchased a book on NLP, I never forgot it and still use it every day!

Neuro-Linguistic Programming (NLP) is a powerful methodology that explores the connection between our thoughts, language, and behaviors. It offers practical techniques and strategies to understand and improve human communication, personal development, and change. NLP provides a framework for identifying and modifying patterns of thought and behavior to enhance personal and professional success. Here is a detailed summary of what NLP is, what it does, and how people can use it:

Here is an overview of what NLP is, how it works, and why you should use it to make decisions:

NLP, or Neuro-Linguistic Programming, is a psychological approach that involves analyzing and modeling human behaviors and thought processes to better understand how we experience the world. The key premise of NLP is that our subjective reality is shaped by our perceptions, and we can intentionally choose to adopt more empowering perceptions that lead to more positive behaviors and outcomes.

At its core, NLP examines how we process information through our senses, filter it through our individual belief systems, and store it in our minds through various representational systems. The primary representational systems are visual, auditory, kinesthetic, olfactory and gustatory. Most people tend to be dominant in one or two of these systems, which determines how we best take in, process, store, recall and make decisions about information.

NLP was developed in the 1970s by Richard Bandler, a mathematician and information scientist, and John Grinder, a linguist. They analyzed and modeled the therapeutic techniques of three pioneers in the field to understand the specific language patterns and behavioral cues that led to successful outcomes: Fritz

Perls (gestalt therapy), Virginia Satir (family systems therapy) and Milton Erickson (hypnotherapy).

What they discovered were subtle but identifiable patterns in how these master therapists structured their sessions, framed problems, used certain words versus others, employed metaphors, paced their speech, used body language, built rapport with clients and utilized trance states. Bandler and Grinder sought to codify these patterns into defined techniques and models that could be learned and applied systematically to improve communication, change perceptions and achieve goals.

Some core NLP techniques include: - Anchoring - Associating a thought, feeling, or behavior with a trigger or "anchor" (visual, auditory, touch) to recall the resourceful state.

- Rapport - Matching and mirroring verbal and nonverbal cues to build mutual understanding and trust.

- Representational systems - Identifying visual, auditory and kinesthetic predicates in language to determine thinking patterns.

- Sensory acuity - Noticing and reading subtle physical cues (e.g., eye movements, breathing changes) to determine the inner experience.

- Pacing and leading - Meeting someone in their model of the world, then influencing change by guiding them to alternative perspectives.

- Parts integration - Identifying and mapping different aspects of self and bringing them into greater alignment.

- Modeling - Replicating strategies used by others to obtain similar results.

- Reframing - Changing the meaning attributed to an event to see it from a more constructive perspective.

- Metaphors - Telling stories that have implicit messages to communicate ideas indirectly at the unconscious level.

- Sub modalities - Adjusting the properties or building blocks of internal representational systems to enhance or diminish responses.

The applications of NLP span many fields, including health, relationships, education, business, law, sports and the performing arts. By better understanding how people process experiences at the cognitive level, there are more possibilities for influencing beneficial changes.

Some examples of using NLP for different goals:

- Managing mental states - Using techniques like anchoring and sub-modalities to shift unwanted emotional reactions and cultivate more resourceful mindsets.

- Motivation - Leveraging visualization to mentally rehearse desired outcomes, cue future behaviors and amplify purpose.

- Habit change - Interrupting limiting patterns and instilling empowering routines by associating them with positive anchors.

- Influence - Building quick rapport, pacing reality and leading to new perceptions to persuasively shift attitudes.

- Communication enhancement - Matching sensory preferences and language styles to improve messaging impact and relationship-building.

- Fear resolution - Identifying and defusing fear triggers by reframing meaning and changing bodily responses.

- Negotiation - Rapport skills and mental flexibility to understand different perspectives and reach collaborative solutions.

- Leadership - Flexible information processing to shift mindsets, motivate teams and drive innovation.

- Learning optimization - Using mental rehearsal and sensory techniques to improve information encoding and recall.

- Health/healing - Visualization, state elicitation and belief change to activate the body's natural healing systems.

- Sports performance - Mental rehearsal, state control and precision in sensory terms to achieve flow states and excellence.

When applied ethically, NLP enhances communication and understanding between people. It provides systemic processes for implementing changes quickly and effectively. NLP empowers people with self-awareness, adaptability and transformative skills to navigate life's challenges.

The most impactful aspect of NLP is that it equips us to master our inner worlds so we can actualize our highest potential. It recognizes that our thoughts, beliefs and mental frameworks shape what is possible. While we cannot always control external events, we have control over our perceptions and responses. NLP gives us deeper influence over our subjective experience of life.

The techniques scaffold in complexity. Anchoring is a simple concept that associates an internal state with a sensory trigger. Reframing reinterprets meaning. Parts integration harmonizes conflicts within the psyche. Modeling extracts and replicates the thinking patterns of excellence. NLP instills self-mastery across cognitive, emotional and behavioral domains.

With its processes and principles, NLP empowers people to:

- Rewrite disempowering narratives

- Transform negative emotional patterns

- Tap into resourceful states on-demand

- Develop greater self-awareness

- Improve interpersonal dynamics

- Let go of limiting assumptions

- Expand behavioral flexibility

- Set empowering goals

- Enrich sensory acuity

- Facilitate generative change

NLP enables thinking that is adaptable, intentional, and aligned with desired outcomes. It gives you tools to decode the thought systems of yourself and others. First-person NLP skills enhance your ability to regulate internal states, beliefs, strategies, and behaviors. Interpersonal NLP skills improve communication, relationships, and influence.

NLP has sometimes gained a bad reputation around manipulation or misuse. However, its core principles are about understanding people better to ethically assist positive change. Used correctly, NLP creates win-win situations. It starts from a place of ecological concern to do no harm.

NLP empowers people with cognitive and behavioral means to become their best selves. It provides technologies to enrich lives. The more we understand NLP principles, the more effectively we can resolve inner conflicts, connect with others, actualize dreams, and maximize personal and collective potential.

In summary, NLP offers a multidisciplinary framework and toolkit to model excellence and optimize human experience. It gives you deeper influence over thoughts, emotions, behaviors, goals, and relationships. NLP helps you intentionally engineer the mental maps that shape your reality. It provides the algorithms to rewrite disempowering life narratives. With NLP, you have a greater capacity to adapt, thrive and self-actualize. So equip yourself with NLP skills to create the life and world you most want to live in.

What does NLP do?

NLP focuses on understanding the ways in which we perceive the world, process information, and create meaning. It explores the impact of language on our thoughts and behaviors and aims to enhance communication, self-awareness, and personal effectiveness. NLP offers a range of techniques to help individuals:

Improve Communication: NLP provides strategies for enhancing communication skills, both with oneself and others.

It offers tools for building rapport, improving listening skills, and effectively expressing ideas and emotions. NLP techniques can be used in various contexts, such as business negotiations, relationships, and personal interactions.

Change Limiting Beliefs: NLP recognizes that our beliefs and perceptions shape our reality. It offers techniques to identify and transform limiting beliefs that hold us back from achieving our goals. By reframing negative beliefs and adopting empowering perspectives, individuals can overcome obstacles and cultivate a positive mindset.

Set Clear Goals: NLP emphasizes the importance of setting well-formed and achievable goals. It provides strategies for clarifying objectives, creating a compelling vision, and designing action plans to accomplish desired outcomes. NLP techniques can help individuals align their conscious and subconscious minds to achieve their goals effectively.

Manage Emotional States: NLP offers techniques for managing and regulating emotions. It provides tools to shift from negative emotional states to more positive ones, promoting emotional well-being and resilience. NLP techniques, such as anchoring and reframing, can help individuals access resourceful emotional states and let go of unhelpful emotions.

Enhance Self-Confidence and Motivation: NLP offers techniques to boost self-confidence, overcome self-doubt, and increase motivation. Through strategies like modeling excellence, visualizations, and affirmations, individuals can develop a strong sense of self-belief and motivation to pursue their goals with determination and enthusiasm.

How can people use NLP?

People can use NLP in various areas of their lives to improve their mindset, communication, and personal effectiveness. Here are some practical ways individuals can apply NLP techniques:

Self-Reflection and Self-Awareness: NLP encourages individuals to observe their thoughts, behaviors, and language patterns. By cultivating self-awareness, individuals can identify patterns that may be holding them back or causing negative outcomes. They can then apply NLP techniques to reframe beliefs, change perspectives, and develop more resourceful ways of thinking.

Effective Communication: NLP provides tools for effective communication, whether in personal or professional settings. Individuals can learn to build rapport, listen actively, and communicate with clarity and influence. NLP techniques can also help individuals adapt their communication style to connect with others more effectively.

Personal Development and Growth: NLP offers a range of techniques for personal development. Individuals can use visualization, affirmations, and goal-setting strategies to clarify their vision, overcome obstacles, and achieve success in various areas of life, such as career, relationships, and health.

Coaching and Therapy: NLP techniques are widely used in coaching and therapy settings. Coaches and therapists utilize NLP tools to help clients overcome limitations, change unwanted behaviors, and achieve their desired outcomes. NLP techniques, such as timeline therapy and parts integration, can facilitate deep personal transformation and healing.

Professional Success: NLP can enhance professional success by improving leadership skills, influencing others, and managing teams effectively. Techniques like modeling successful individuals, understanding different communication styles, and managing emotions can support individuals in achieving career advancement and excellence.

NLP is a versatile methodology that offers practical techniques and strategies for personal growth, communication, and change. By understanding the power of language, thought patterns, and beliefs, individuals can apply NLP techniques to enhance their mindset, improve communication skills, and achieve their goals. NLP empowers individuals to take charge of their thoughts and behaviors, leading to greater self-awareness, personal effectiveness, and overall well-being.

Here are three highly regarded books on NLP that provide valuable insights and practical techniques:

"The Structure of Magic I: A Book About Language and Therapy" by Richard Bandler and John Grinder:

This classic book introduces the foundational principles of NLP. Bandler and Grinder, the co-founders of NLP, explore the patterns and structure of effective communication, focusing on the language used in therapy sessions. The book provides insights into the techniques and strategies that form the basis of NLP, making it a must-read for anyone interested in understanding the core concepts of NLP.

"Frogs into Princes: Neuro Linguistic Programming" by Richard Bandler and John Grinder:

In this influential book, Bandler and Grinder delve into the practical applications of NLP. They share a series of seminars where they demonstrate NLP techniques and discuss the underlying principles. The book covers various NLP topics, including rapport building, sensory acuity, reframing, and the use of language to effect change. "Frogs into Princes" offers a comprehensive introduction to NLP techniques and their potential for personal transformation.

"NLP: The New Technology of Achievement" by Steve Andreas and Charles Faulkner:

This book provides a comprehensive overview of NLP techniques and their application in various aspects of life. Andreas and Faulkner offer practical exercises, case studies, and step-by-step instructions for using NLP to improve communication, set and achieve goals, build self-confidence, and enhance personal effectiveness. "NLP: The New Technology of Achievement" is a user-friendly guide that combines theory with actionable strategies, making it accessible to both beginners and those familiar with NLP.

These books offer valuable insights and techniques for individuals interested in exploring NLP and applying its principles to enhance personal growth, communication, and success.

5 Mind Technique Experiments

Here are detailed answers for each technique, explaining how they are performed and their benefits:

Affirmations: Affirmations are positive statements that help reframe your thoughts and beliefs. They can be used to counteract negative self-talk and instill empowering beliefs in your subconscious mind. Here's how you can perform affirmations effectively:

(a) Choose to empower statements: Select affirmations that resonate with you and align with your goals and values. They should be positive, present tense, and specific. For example, "I am confident and capable," "I embrace positivity in every aspect of my life," or "I am deserving of love and happiness."

(b) Repeat affirmations regularly: Set aside dedicated time each day to repeat your affirmations. You can say them aloud, write them down, or use visualization techniques to reinforce their impact. Aim for consistency and repetition to internalize the positive messages.

(c) Engage your emotions: As you recite or write your affirmations, connect with the emotions associated with them. Feel the positive energy and belief behind each statement. Emotionally engaging with your affirmations enhances their effectiveness and helps rewire your thought patterns.

(d) Personalize affirmations: Tailor affirmations to your unique circumstances and challenges. Address specific areas of your life where you want to cultivate a positive mindset. For example, if you struggle with self-confidence in public speaking, your affirmation can be, "I confidently express myself and captivate my audience with ease."

The benefits of affirmations include: Shifting negative thought patterns: Affirmations replace negative self-talk with positive and empowering beliefs, allowing you to reframe your mindset and build self-confidence.

Increasing self-belief: By consistently repeating affirmations, you reinforce positive beliefs about yourself and your capabilities. This boosts self-esteem and self-efficacy.

Enhancing motivation: Affirmations help you stay focused on your goals and maintain a positive outlook, increasing your motivation and drive to take action.

Cultivating resilience: During challenging times, affirmations can provide encouragement and support, reminding you of your strengths and ability to overcome obstacles.

Improving self-awareness: Engaging in affirmations requires self-reflection and introspection. It helps you become more aware of your thought patterns, allowing you to consciously replace negative thoughts with positive ones.

Gratitude Practice: Cultivating gratitude involves focusing on and appreciating the positive aspects of your life. It promotes a shift in perspective from what's lacking to what's already present. Here's how you can perform a gratitude practice effectively:

(a) Daily reflection: Set aside a few minutes each day to reflect on the things you are grateful for. It can be done in the morning to start your day on a positive note, or in the evening to reflect on the day's blessings.

(b) List or journal: Write down the things you are grateful for in a journal or create a gratitude list. Be specific and detailed, expressing appreciation for both big and small blessings. For example, you can express gratitude for supportive relationships, good health, nature's beauty, or personal achievements.

(c) Practice mindfulness: While reflecting on gratitude, bring your full attention to the present moment. Engage your senses and notice the positive experiences or blessings in your surroundings. This helps anchor your gratitude practice in the present reality.

(d) Express gratitude to others: Extend your gratitude beyond personal reflection by expressing appreciation to the people in your life. It can be a heartfelt thank-you note, a kind word, or acts of kindness that show your gratitude.

The benefits of a gratitude practice include: Increased happiness and well-being: Focusing on gratitude shifts your attention towards positive aspects of your life, fostering a sense of contentment and happiness.

Improved mental health: Gratitude has been linked to reducing symptoms of depression, anxiety, and stress. It helps cultivate a positive mindset and resilience.

Strengthened relationships: Expressing gratitude to others deepens connections, fosters positivity, and strengthens bonds.

Heightened self-awareness: Regularly practicing gratitude enhances your ability to notice and appreciate the present moment and the good things in your life.

Greater optimism: Gratitude practice helps develop an optimistic outlook, enabling you to perceive and approach challenges with a positive mindset.

Visualization: Visualization involves creating vivid mental images of desired outcomes or positive experiences. It harnesses the power of imagination to enhance performance, confidence, and motivation. Here's how you can practice visualization effectively:

(a) Relaxation and focus: Find a quiet and comfortable space where you can relax without distractions. Close your eyes and take a few deep breaths to center yourself. Release any tension or stress in your body.

(b) Set a clear intention: Identify a specific goal or desired outcome you want to visualize. Whether it's achieving a personal milestone, succeeding in a particular endeavor, or overcoming a challenge, define your intention clearly in your mind.

(c) Engage your senses: Visualize the scenario in vivid detail, engaging all your senses. Imagine the sights, sounds, smells, tastes, and tactile sensations associated with your desired outcome. The more detailed and sensory-rich your visualization, the more impactful it becomes.

(d) Embrace positive emotions: As you visualize, immerse yourself in positive emotions related to your desired outcome. Feel the joy, confidence, and satisfaction that arise from achieving your goal. Allow these emotions to fill you up and become an integral part of your visualization.

(e) Repeat and practice regularly: Make visualization a regular practice, incorporating it into your daily routine. Set aside dedicated time each day to engage in your visualization practice. The more frequently you engage in visualization, the more effective it becomes.

The benefits of visualization include:

Improved performance: Visualization enhances mental rehearsal and prepares you for success. By vividly imagining yourself performing at your best, you strengthen the neural connections associated with the desired actions, leading to improved performance.

Increased confidence: Visualizing success boosts confidence and self-belief. It allows you to experience success in your mind before it happens in reality, reinforcing positive expectations.

Enhanced motivation: Visualization connects you with the emotions and drive associated with your goals. It keeps you motivated, focused, and committed to taking the necessary actions to achieve your desired outcomes.

Stress reduction: Engaging in visualization helps reduce anxiety and stress by creating a mental space of calmness, confidence, and control.

Improved problem-solving: Visualization can be used to mentally rehearse overcoming challenges or finding solutions to obstacles. It enhances your problem-solving skills and increases adaptability in real-life situations.

Positive Self-Talk: Positive self-talk involves consciously replacing negative or self-deprecating thoughts with positive and empowering statements. It's a powerful tool for reshaping your internal dialogue and cultivating a more positive mindset. Here's how you can practice positive self-talk effectively:

(a) Identify negative self-talk: Begin by becoming aware of your negative self-talk patterns. Notice when self-critical or self-defeating thoughts arise in your mind.

(b) Challenge negative thoughts: Whenever a negative thought arises, challenge its validity. Ask yourself if there is evidence to support or refute the negative belief. Often, negative thoughts are based on assumptions or distorted thinking.

(c) Reframe negative thoughts: Once you've challenged negative thoughts, reframe them into positive and empowering statements. For example, if you catch yourself thinking, "I always mess things up," reframe it as, "I am learning and growing from my mistakes, and I can do better next time."

(d) Replace negative with positive: Consciously replace negative self-talk with positive affirmations and encouraging statements. Repeat these positive statements to yourself whenever negative thoughts arise. Over time, this helps rewire your thought patterns.

(e) Practice self-compassion: Be kind and compassionate towards yourself. Treat yourself with the same level of care and support that you would offer to a friend. Encourage and uplift yourself through positive self-talk.

The benefits of positive self-talk include: Improved self-esteem: Positive self-talk builds a foundation of self-worth and self-acceptance. It helps you develop a positive perception of yourself and your abilities.

Increased self-confidence: By replacing self-doubt with self-assurance, positive self-talk boosts your confidence and belief in your capabilities.

Reduced stress and anxiety: Positive self-talk counteracts negative thoughts that contribute to stress and anxiety. It promotes relaxation and a sense of calm.

Enhanced problem-solving: Positive self-talk enables you to approach challenges with a constructive mindset, fostering creative problem-solving skills.

Improved resilience: By reframing setbacks and failures as learning opportunities, positive self-talk helps build resilience and bounce back from difficulties.

Mindfulness and Meditation: Mindfulness and meditation practices involve bringing your attention to the present moment, cultivating awareness, and accepting your thoughts and emotions without judgment. These practices foster a calm and centered state of mind. Here's how you can incorporate mindfulness and meditation into your daily life:

(a) Set aside dedicated time: Allocate a specific time each day for mindfulness and meditation practice. Start with shorter sessions and gradually increase the duration as you become more comfortable.

(b) Find a quiet space: Choose a quiet and comfortable space where you won't be disturbed. Create an environment that supports relaxation and focus.

(c) Begin with deep breathing: Start your practice with a few deep breaths to anchor yourself in the present moment. Pay attention to the sensation of your breath entering and leaving your body.

(d) Focus on the present moment: Shift your attention to the present moment and observe your thoughts, emotions, and bodily sensations without judgment. Notice the thoughts as they come and go, without getting caught up in them.

(e) Cultivate non-judgmental awareness: Practice observing your thoughts and emotions with a sense of curiosity and acceptance. Avoid labeling them as good or bad, but simply acknowledge their presence.

(f) Return to the breath: Whenever you notice your mind wandering, gently guide your attention back to your breath. Use the breath as an anchor to bring you back to the present moment.

(g) Expand mindfulness to daily activities: Extend mindfulness beyond formal meditation sessions and bring it into your daily activities. Engage fully in each moment, whether it's eating, walking, or conversing with others.

The benefits of mindfulness and meditation include: Stress reduction: Mindfulness practices promote relaxation and reduce the impact of stress on the body and mind. They help you cultivate a sense of calm and equanimity.

Improved focus and concentration: Regular mindfulness practice enhances focus and concentration, allowing you to be more present and attentive in your daily life.

Emotional regulation: Mindfulness helps you observe and accept your emotions without judgment, leading to improved emotional well-being and regulation.

Increased self-awareness: By observing your thoughts and emotions, mindfulness deepens your self-awareness and understanding of your internal experiences.

Enhanced resilience: Mindfulness strengthens your ability to navigate challenges and bounce back from setbacks by fostering a non-reactive and accepting attitude towards difficulties.

Remember that these techniques require consistent practice and patience. Experiment with them and find what resonates with you the most. Incorporating these practices into your daily routine can lead to a more positive mindset, improved well-being, and a greater ability to navigate life's challenges with grace and resilience.

Simple NLP Techniques to Practice Everyday

1. Use sensory awareness - Tune into the sights, sounds, textures, tastes and smells around you to become more present and attuned to the environment. For instance, when drinking coffee, notice the aroma, flavor, and warmth of the cup in your hands.

2. Observe eye accessing cues - Notice which direction people look when recalling experiences or constructing thoughts to understand their thinking patterns. If someone looks up and to the left when describing a memory, they are likely accessing a visually constructed image.

3. Match and mirror - Align your posture, gestures, voice tone, speed, and breathing with someone to build quick rapport. If they lean in when speaking, reciprocate by leaning in.

4. Use predicates - Listen for sensory words people use to represent information like "see" for visual, "hear" for auditory or "feel" for kinesthetic to determine modalities. Ask questions and frame messages accordingly.

5. Vary representational systems - Describe ideas using imagery, sounds, textures or actions so information lands clearly for different learning styles. For instance, portray a beach scene using visual details, the sound of waves and the feeling of sand.

6. Get outcome oriented - Identify the tangible result you want to achieve in any situation to get clarity and direction. Whether it's a work milestone or household task, define the end goal.

7. Set well-formed outcomes - Shape desired results that are: stated in the positive, initiated and maintained by self, sensory-specific, contextually appropriate, and achievable through action. "I easily complete this report by 3pm today."

8. Break tasks into steps - Map out the sequence of smaller actions needed to accomplish a goal. To write a book, steps include: outlining chapters, writing daily word count, getting feedback on drafts, submitting to publishers.

9. Use future pacing - Imagine you have already achieved an outcome successfully to embody the accomplishment and positive emotions. See, hear and feel the experience vividly. Celebrate in your mind.

10. Model excellence - Study people who excel in areas you want to improve in. What mindsets, qualities, habits, and strategies do they embody? Apply what you learn.

11. Detach from un-resourceful states - Notice negative emotions, limiting beliefs or unhelpful patterns as transient rather than who you are. They pass through; you remain.

12. Utilize reframing - Change the meaning you assign events to perceive from empowering perspectives. A problem becomes an opportunity to learn. A mistake is feedback to grow.

13. Forgive others and self - Release resentment and blame to shift from past hurts into acceptance and peace through understanding people's humanity. Focus on the future.

14. Meditate - Practice calming your mind, focusing attention, and entering a relaxed yet alert state to reduce stress, develop equanimity, and tap intuition.

15. Express gratitude - Appreciate life's gifts, both big and small. Thank others who have helped you. Savor and acknowledge the positive as an antidote to negative mindsets.

16. Find the learning - Ask "what can I learn?" in challenging circumstances rather than getting stuck in reactions. Gain wisdom from hardships and failures.

17. Identify resources - Remember peak states, talents, values, and accomplishments you have accessed before to tap into them again. Draw strength from your proven inner reserves.

18. Set milestones - Create smaller, progressive subgoals along the path toward major life goals. Getting a degree may involve steps like passing core classes, choosing a major, applying for a program, graduating.

19. Use rituals - Develop personal routines that mindfully ground you and provide structure to your day, week or season, like meditation, exercise, reflection. Ritualize change to solidify new habits.

20. Speak positively - Phrase suggestions or instructions using positive language about what you want someone to do rather than negative phrasing about the problem. "Walk slowly and breathe deeply" versus "don't panic."

21. Ask empowering questions - Guide your thinking by asking solution-focused questions: What outcome do I want? What action steps can I take? Who can assist me? How can I stay motivated?

22. Manage state - Use triggers like music, images, affirmations or physical postures to induce desired emotional states like confidence before a presentation.

23. Develop peripheral vision - Broaden your attention to absorb more information from your environment. Cast a wider net of sensory awareness to enrich perspective and insight.

24. Believe in yourself - Replace doubts with affirming self-talk. Recall past successes. Focus on strengths. Cultivate self-trust. Expect the best to activate courage and achievement.

25. Find common ground - When relating, establish rapport by highlighting shared values and interests to generate goodwill and cooperation.

26. Lead by example - Model the mindsets and behaviors you seek to inspire in others. Practice patience, optimism, and purpose. Walk your talk.

27. Provide feedback gracefully - Frame suggestions positively and descriptively. Offer new learnings to consider, not judgments. Provide feedback to help people flourish.

28. Negotiate win-win deals - Listen to understand all parties' interests to create solutions where shared goals are met. Collaborate rather than compete.

29. Develop emotional intelligence - Carefully observe your inner landscape. Become fluent in reading your feelings and needs so you can express them constructively.

30. Cultivate whole-body intelligence - Sharpen your senses. Notice how decisions affect energy levels long-term. Integrate logic and intuition. Let head and heart inform each other.

31. Balance antagonist polarities - Blend opposing qualities like courage and consideration, accountability and compassion. Avoid either-or thinking.

32. Strategize success - Clarify big picture vision, analyze current reality, brainstorm methods, identify resources, take action. Regularly refine approach.

33. Structure time effectively - Cluster similar tasks to maximize focus. Take breaks to renew energy. Schedule priorities first before less important items.

34. Increase learning agility - Proactively seek new knowledge, skills, and feedback. Be willing to question assumptions and change course as situations evolve.

35. Develop resilience - Rebound from setbacks by reframing problems into opportunities, staying focused deliberately, and drawing strength from your self-concept.

36. Turn mistakes into lessons - View failures and mistakes as feedback to hone skills and judgment, not as proof of inadequacy. Extract the wisdom, then let go.

37. Reinforce changes - To actualize new habits, anchor them to vividly imagined rewards. Create reminders and accountabilities. Celebrate small successes.

38. Influence ethically - Seek to understand people's reasoning and desired outcomes. Present win-win solutions focused on their gain, not manipulation.

39. Unleash creativity - Diverge by brainstorming wildly without judgment. Converge by evaluating possibilities and combining options. Allow originality to flourish.

40. Envision success vividly - Use all your senses to mentally rehearse attainment of goals. Picture crossing finish lines, receiving awards, achieving aims as if living it now.

41. Find the blessing - Even in difficulties, look for the upside. How can this problem strengthen me? Improve a relationship? Develop my abilities? Generate new possibilities?

42. Transform concerns - Reframe emotional upsets as messengers of your deeper needs and values. Let go of reacting to focus on responding helpfully.

43. Lighten up - Don't take yourself too seriously. Cultivate the ability to laugh at mistakes and see humor in absurdities. Take playful breaks.

44. Value relationships - Nurture connection, belonging, and intimacy needs. Prioritize people over things. Express affection. Share joys.

45. Contribute - Uplift others with small acts of kindness, compassion, and service. Volunteer. Donate. Stand up for justice. Make a difference.

46. Live purposefully - Clarify and act on values. Align daily choices with what matters most: helping people, learning, creativity, peace, nobility.

47. Develop self-awareness - Pause frequently to notice thoughts, feelings, and behaviors. Observe, but don't over-identify with passing contents of consciousness.

48. Cultivate response-ability - Pause when reactive. Consider the best response. Act and speak from wisdom, not impulse. Choose empowerment over victim thinking.

49. Let go and trust - Release rather than resist. Be present. Have faith in life's unfolding. Surrender unnecessary control and perfectionism.

50. Awaken each morning - Begin the day meditating for centering, envisioning purpose, and setting empowering intentions. Create a positive tone.

In summary, keep it simple. NLP offers basic techniques to enrich moment-to-moment living - from enhancing your senses to shaping your inner talk. Put these principles into consistent practice to develop helpful life skills leading to greater flourishing and fulfillment.

Visualization: Seeing Success Before it Happens

Visualization is a powerful technique that involves creating mental images or representations of concepts, ideas, or data. It leverages the brain's ability to process and understand visual information more effectively than textual or numerical data alone. Visualization can be used in various fields, including art, design, science, and personal development. This technique allows individuals to explore and understand complex information, gain insights, and communicate ideas more efficiently.

The goal of visualization can vary depending on the context. It could be to solve a problem, understand relationships, make informed decisions, or communicate information effectively. Regardless of the specific objective, visualization involves transforming abstract or complex data into visual representations that are easier to comprehend and work with.

To achieve your goal using visualization, follow these steps: Define your objective: Begin by clarifying what you want to accomplish through visualization. Are you trying to understand a complex concept, communicate information to others, or explore patterns in data? Clearly defining your goal will guide your visualization process.

Gather relevant data: Collect the data that you will use for visualization. This could include numerical data, text, images, or any other relevant information. Ensure that the data is accurate, complete, and reliable.

Choose an appropriate visualization method: There are numerous visualization techniques available, ranging from simple charts and graphs to more advanced 3D modeling and interactive visualizations. Select the method that best suits your data and goal. For example, if you want to showcase trends over time, a line chart might be suitable. If you intend to compare categories, a bar chart could be more appropriate. If you're working with geographic data, a map visualization might be the best choice.

Design your visualization: Once you have selected the visualization method, design the visual representation. Consider the aesthetics, layout, colors, and labels. Ensure that your visualization is visually appealing and easy to interpret. Use appropriate visual cues such as color, size, and shape to convey meaning and highlight important information.

Create the visualization: Using software tools specifically designed for data visualization, such as Tableau, Excel, or Python libraries like Matplotlib or D3.js, implement your design. Input your data into the chosen tool and apply the appropriate settings to generate the visualization. Experiment with different settings to refine the visualization until it effectively communicates the desired information.

Interpret the visualization: Once your visualization is created, carefully analyze and interpret the visual representation. Search for patterns, trends, and relationships within the data. Consider the insights that the visualization provides and how they relate to your initial goal. Visualization helps to identify patterns and outliers that might not be immediately apparent in raw data.

Communicate and share: Visualization is a powerful tool for communication. Use your visualization to convey your findings, insights, or ideas to others. Present your visualization in a clear and concise manner, ensuring that your audience can understand the information you are trying to convey. Consider adding annotations, labels, or a narrative to guide the viewer's understanding.

Iterate and refine: Visualization is an iterative process. As you gather feedback, continue to refine your visualization to make it more effective and impactful. Experiment with different visual representations, or adjust design elements based on feedback or new insights that emerge.

By following these steps, you can harness the power of visualization to achieve your goals. Visualization allows you to explore complex information, gain insights, and communicate effectively. Whether you're trying to understand data, communicate ideas, or solve problems, visualization is a valuable technique that can enhance your understanding and help you achieve your objectives.

Many successful people have used visualization techniques to achieve their goals and attain success. Here are a few examples:

Jim Carrey: The renowned actor and comedian, Jim Carrey, is known for using visualization to manifest his dreams. Before achieving fame and fortune, Carrey would write himself a check for $10 million for "acting services rendered" and carry it in his wallet. He would visualize himself receiving the payment and achieving his career goals. Eventually, Carrey received a movie role that paid him exactly $10 million, which he attributes to the power of visualization.

Oprah Winfrey: Media mogul Oprah Winfrey is a strong believer in the power of visualization. She has credited visualization as a key factor in her success. Winfrey would visualize her goals and envision herself achieving them, which helped her stay focused and motivated. She often discusses the importance of creating a vision board to help clarify and manifest her desires.

Arnold Schwarzenegger: The legendary bodybuilder, actor, and politician, Arnold Schwarzenegger, is known for using visualization techniques throughout his career. He would visualize himself winning bodybuilding competitions, envision his future success in Hollywood, and imagine himself as a successful politician. Schwarzenegger believes that visualization played a significant role in his accomplishments.

Conor McGregor: The mixed martial artist Conor McGregor has spoken about using visualization as a crucial part of his training and mental preparation. He would visualize himself winning fights, landing specific punches, and achieving his desired outcomes. McGregor credits visualization for helping him build confidence and focus, which contributed to his success in the world of combat sports.

Serena Williams: Tennis superstar Serena Williams has used visualization techniques to enhance her performance on the court. Williams would visualize herself hitting perfect shots, winning matches, and holding championship trophies. By mentally rehearsing her success, Williams believes she was able to expand her skills and overcome challenges.

These are just a few examples, but there are many more successful individuals who have incorporated visualization techniques into their lives to help them achieve their goals and reach their full potential.

Positive Visualization Example

Positive visualization can greatly benefit a weightlifting athlete who is striving to achieve a record in his weight class. By engaging in vivid and positive mental imagery, the athlete can enhance his performance, boost confidence, and increase the likelihood of reaching his goal. Here's a detailed explanation of how positive visualization can help him:

Mental Rehearsal: Positive visualization involves mentally rehearsing the desired outcome, imagining the entire process of successfully lifting the weight and breaking the record. The athlete can visualize himself stepping onto the platform with confidence, positioning himself for the lift, and executing the technique flawlessly. By repeatedly visualizing this successful scenario, the athlete's mind becomes familiar with the movements and builds a sense of confidence and familiarity.

Enhancing Focus and Concentration: Positive visualization helps the athlete enhance focus and concentration during training and competitions. By picturing himself lifting the weight successfully, the athlete can eliminate distractions and stay fully present in the moment. Visualizing the details, such as the grip on the bar, the body positioning, and the sound of the crowd, helps the athlete immerse himself in the experience and block out any negative or distracting thoughts.

Increasing Confidence: Positive visualization cultivates a strong sense of self-belief and confidence. The athlete mentally rehearses the successful lift, reinforcing the belief that he is capable of achieving the record. By repeatedly visualizing success, the athlete's subconscious mind internalizes the image of accomplishment, boosting confidence levels. This increased confidence translates into a positive mindset, allowing the athlete to approach the lift with greater self-assurance and determination.

Managing Anxiety and Pressure: Visualizing success in a calm and controlled manner helps the athlete manage anxiety and pressure. The mental rehearsal of the lift, combined with positive emotions and sensations, helps reduce performance anxiety and pre-competition nerves. The athlete can use positive visualization techniques to create a mental state of calmness and focus, allowing him to channel his energy effectively during the lift and stay composed under pressure.

Developing Motor Patterns and Technique: Positive visualization assists in refining and perfecting the athlete's motor patterns and technique. By visualizing the lift in detail, including the correct body mechanics, muscle engagement, and movement sequencing, the athlete reinforces proper technique in his mind. This mental rehearsal helps create neural pathways and strengthens the mind-muscle connection, enhancing the athlete's ability to execute the lift optimally during actual performance.

Overcoming Challenges and Obstacles: Positive visualization prepares the athlete to overcome challenges and obstacles that may arise during the lift. By mentally rehearsing different scenarios, such as encountering resistance or experiencing fatigue, the athlete can strategize and develop coping mechanisms in advance. Visualizing successful problem-solving and adapting to unexpected situations helps the athlete build resilience and confidence in his ability to overcome obstacles during the lift.

Harnessing Motivation and Drive: Positive visualization taps into the athlete's motivation and drive to succeed. By picturing himself breaking the record and experiencing the thrill of accomplishment, the athlete fuels his internal motivation. Visualizing the end goal and the satisfaction that comes with achieving it reinforces the athlete's determination and drive to put in the necessary effort during training and competitions.

Improving Performance Consistency: Positive visualization contributes to improved performance consistency. By consistently engaging in positive mental imagery, the athlete conditions his mind to expect success and maintain a positive mindset. This consistency translates into more consistent physical performance, as the athlete approaches each lift with a confident and focused mindset, regardless of external factors or distractions.

Increasing Resilience and Grit: Positive visualization cultivates resilience and grit within the athlete. By visualizing successful outcomes and persevering through mental challenges, the athlete develops mental toughness. This resilience allows the athlete to push through fatigue, setbacks, and failures, maintaining a positive outlook and continuing to strive for the record despite any temporary setbacks.

Building a Positive Feedback Loop: Positive visualization creates a positive feedback loop between the mind and body. As the athlete visualizes success, positive emotions and sensations are associated with the imagined lift. These positive feelings create a physiological response, such as increased confidence, relaxation, and heightened focus. This positive feedback loop reinforces the athlete's positive mindset and primes the body for optimal performance during the actual lift.

Positive visualization can significantly contribute to an athlete's success in weightlifting by enhancing focus, confidence, technique, resilience, and overall performance. By consistently engaging in positive mental imagery, the athlete prepares his mind and body for success, increasing the likelihood of achieving his goal of breaking the record in his weight class.

Willpower is Mind Power

What is Willpower?

Willpower is defined as the ability to control one's thoughts, emotions, and behaviors to resist temptations and impulses and work toward longer-term goals. It requires self-discipline, motivation, and focus to override immediate desires that conflict with deeper values and priorities. Willpower allows people to make choices aligned with their aspirations rather than giving in to distractions or indulgences.

Willpower is sometimes called self-control or self-regulation. It is a form of mental energy that can be depleted but also strengthened over time. Willpower functions like a muscle—with regular exercise, it fatigues less easily. But when willpower reserves run low, it becomes harder to say no to temptation. For this reason, people need to conserve willpower and replenish it through proper rest, nutrition, and stress management.

The key components of willpower include

Attention Control - Focusing on goal-relevant information and ignoring distractions. This involves filtering out irrelevant stimuli and concentrating mental resources on what matters most. Meditation and mindfulness build attention control.

Cognitive Restructuring - Reframing situations and urges in ways that reduce their power over us. For example, viewing a tempting cookie as a threat rather than a treat.

Impulse Control - Resisting automatic or conditioned responses to make deliberate, conscious choices aligned with objectives and values. Taking a moment before reacting helps improve impulse control.

Emotional Regulation - Handling feelings that might derail efforts, like frustration, anxiety, or boredom. Strategies include acknowledging, allowing, and adapting emotions.

Delayed Gratification - Forgoing immediate pleasure for greater future rewards. Visualizing long-term benefits, keeping rewards out of sight, and pre-committing to restraint are useful techniques.

Stress Resilience - Managing stress is key to preserving willpower. Healthy habits like exercise, sleep, and social connection replenish willpower reserves.

There are several key theories and models that provide frameworks for understanding willpower:

Ego Depletion - This posits that willpower is finite and gets used up with effortful thinking and difficult choices. Conserving willpower by limiting daily demands allows greater self-control in key moments.

Process Model - This focuses on motivational factors underpinning willpower, emphasizing desire for goals over resistance of temptation. Reframing rewards boosts motivation.

Opponent-Process Theory - This looks at willpower as a constantly shifting balance between competing impulses and self-discipline that ultimately strengthens with repeated practice.

Strength Model - This views willpower as an energy that can grow stronger over time, similar to a muscle. Regular small efforts to build self-control expand willpower reserves.

In summary, willpower relies on several interconnected cognitive processes and mental skills that can be built up intentionally. While it depletes in the short-term, nurturing motivation, managing stress, practicing discipline, and structuring choices all strengthen willpower over time. Awareness and utilization of willpower techniques can help achieve meaningful goals.

Willpower can be considered a facet of mind power, as it involves the ability to exert control over one's thoughts, emotions, and actions. However, it's important to note that the mind encompasses a broader range of cognitive functions and processes beyond just willpower.

The mind plays a crucial role in directing a person to use their will. It involves a combination of mental processes, such as motivation, decision-making, and self-control. Here's a general overview of how the mind influences the use of will:

Setting goals: The mind helps individuals define and establish their goals, whether short-term or long-term. By clarifying their objectives, individuals create a mental framework that guides their actions.

Motivation: The mind generates motivation, which fuels the desire and determination to achieve those goals. Motivation can come from external factors, such as rewards or recognition, or internal factors, like personal values or aspirations.

Focus and concentration: The mind helps individuals direct their attention and concentrate on tasks relevant to their goals. Maintaining focus enables individuals to resist distractions and stay committed to their chosen course of action.

Decision-making: The mind evaluates choices and makes decisions based on factors like priorities, values, and available information. Willpower comes into play when individuals make choices aligned with their goals, even if it requires resisting immediate gratification or overcoming obstacles.

Self-control: The mind enables individuals to regulate their thoughts, emotions, and behaviors. Willpower is particularly relevant in exercising self-control, as it involves overriding impulsive or habitual responses in favor of more beneficial actions.

Persistence and resilience: The mind provides individuals with the mental fortitude to persist in the face of challenges and setbacks. Willpower helps individuals stay determined, bounce back from failures, and maintain their efforts over time.

Mental rehearsal and visualization: The mind can employ techniques like mental rehearsal and visualization to enhance willpower. By mentally rehearsing success or visualizing the desired outcome, individuals strengthen their resolve and increase their belief in their ability to achieve their goals.

It's important to note that willpower can vary among individuals, and it can be strengthened and developed through practice and conscious effort. By understanding how the mind influences willpower, individuals can cultivate their ability to use their will effectively and achieve their desired outcomes.

Breathing

Proper breathing is essential for meditation and relaxation as it helps calm the mind, reduce stress, and promote a sense of tranquility. Here's a detailed explanation of proper breathing techniques for meditation and relaxation:

Deep Abdominal Breathing: This technique involves breathing deeply into your abdomen rather than shallowly into your chest. Start by sitting or lying down in a comfortable position. Place one hand on your abdomen and the other on your chest. Inhale slowly through your nose, allowing your abdomen to rise and expand. Feel the breath filling your lower lungs, pushing your diaphragm downward. Exhale gently through your nose or mouth, allowing your abdomen to fall naturally. Focus on the sensation of your breath and the rise and fall of your abdomen with each inhalation and exhalation.

Diaphragmatic Breathing: Diaphragmatic breathing, also known as belly breathing, activates the diaphragm muscle and promotes deep relaxation. Sit or lie down comfortably. Place one hand on your chest and the other on your abdomen. Take a slow, deep breath in through your nose, allowing your abdomen to rise as you fill your lower lungs. As you exhale, gently contract your abdominal muscles, allowing your abdomen to fall naturally. Focus on the movement of your diaphragm and the sensation of deep, rhythmic breathing.

Equal Breathing (Sama Vritti): This technique involves equalizing the length of your inhalations and exhalations. Find a comfortable position and begin to breathe in and out through your nose. Inhale for a count of four, then exhale for a count of four. Keep the length of your inhalation and exhalation equal. As you become more comfortable, you can gradually increase the count to six, eight, or even ten. This technique helps balance the nervous system and promotes a sense of calm and focus.

Box Breathing: Box breathing, also known as square breathing, is a technique that involves equalizing the length of your inhalations, retentions, exhalations, and pauses. Imagine tracing a square shape as you breathe. Inhale slowly for a count of four, hold your breath for a count of four, exhale for a count of four, and then hold your breath again for a count of four. Repeat this cycle several times, focusing on the smooth and steady flow of your breath.

Mindful Breathing: Mindful breathing involves simply observing your breath without trying to control or change it. Find a comfortable position and bring your attention to your breath. Notice the sensation of the breath as it enters and leaves your body. Observe the rise and fall of your abdomen or the feeling of air passing through your nostrils. If your mind wanders, gently bring your focus back to your breath without judgment. This technique cultivates present-moment awareness and helps calm the mind.

Remember, proper breathing for meditation and relaxation is about cultivating a sense of ease and tranquility. Experiment with different techniques and find the one that resonates with you the most. Regular practice will help you develop a deeper connection with your breath and enhance your ability to relax and enter a meditative state.

The Mozart Music Effect on Our Minds

To this day, even as I write this, I use this unbelievable trick. Nothing can clear the mind like the old-world classical works.

The phenomenon known as the "Mozart effect" refers to the idea that listening to Mozart's music can have a positive impact on cognitive abilities and the mind. The concept gained popularity after a study conducted in 1993 by researchers at the University of California, Irvine, led by Dr. Frances Rauscher.

In the study, participants listened to either a Mozart sonata, a relaxation tape, or silence for ten minutes. Afterward, they were assessed on spatial-temporal reasoning, which involves understanding and manipulating visual and spatial relationships. The results showed that participants who listened to Mozart's music performed significantly better on these tasks compared to the other groups.

This finding led to the notion that Mozart's music has a specific effect on the brain, enhancing cognitive functioning and spatial-temporal abilities. However, it's important to note that the Mozart effect is temporary and doesn't imply a permanent increase in intelligence or long-term cognitive benefits. Since the initial study, further research has been conducted to explore the Mozart effect and its underlying mechanisms. One hypothesis suggests that the complex and structured nature of Mozart's compositions may stimulate neural pathways related to cognitive processing and spatial reasoning.

Additionally, listening to music, including Mozart's, has been found to have various effects on the mind and mental well-being. Music has the ability to evoke emotions, stimulate memories, and create a sense of relaxation or excitement. It can also influence physiological responses, such as heart rate and blood pressure.

Engaging with music, including Mozart's compositions, has been associated with several mental benefits, such as:

Mood enhancement: Music can evoke positive emotions and uplift the mood. Listening to Mozart's music, with its beautiful melodies and harmonies, can promote a sense of joy and tranquility.

Stress reduction: Music has the power to induce relaxation and reduce stress levels. The soothing qualities of Mozart's compositions can help calm the mind and alleviate tension.

Improved focus and concentration: Music can enhance cognitive function and aid in concentration. Certain compositions, including those by Mozart, are often recommended as background music for studying or working due to their potential to enhance focus.

Emotional expression: Listening to music, including Mozart's works, provides a means for emotional expression and release. It can help individuals connect with and process their emotions, promoting mental well-being.

Cognitive stimulation: Engaging with complex musical pieces, such as Mozart's symphonies or piano concertos, can stimulate cognitive processes, including attention, memory, and problem-solving skills.

While the specific mechanisms underlying the connection between Mozart's music and the mind are still being explored, it's evident that music, including his compositions, can have profound effects on mental states, emotions, and cognitive abilities. So, whether you're seeking relaxation, inspiration, or cognitive stimulation, indulging in the beauty of Mozart's music can be a delightful and enriching experience for the mind.

Additional Music

Besides Mozart, there have been studies exploring the effects of music by other composers on the mind and cognitive abilities. While the "Mozart effect" is perhaps the most well-known, research has expanded to investigate the impact of various types of music and different composers. Here are a few examples:

Baroque Music: The music of Baroque composers like Johann Sebastian Bach and Antonio Vivaldi has been found to have positive effects on cognitive function. Studies have shown that listening to Baroque music, with its complex and structured compositions, can improve focus, attention, and memory.

Ambient and New Age Music: Ambient and New Age music, characterized by soothing sounds and gentle melodies, has been associated with relaxation and stress reduction. These genres, often featuring calming synthesizer sounds and nature-inspired themes, can promote a tranquil mental state and aid in meditation or relaxation practices.

Classical Music in General: While Mozart's music has received significant attention, studies have shown that listening to classical music in general can have positive effects on the mind. Works by composers such as Ludwig van Beethoven, Wolfgang Amadeus Mozart, Johann Strauss II, and many others have been found to enhance mood, reduce stress, and improve cognitive performance.

Nature Sounds and Instrumental Music: Beyond specific composers, nature sounds and instrumental music have also been explored for their impact on the mind. The sounds of nature, such as flowing water, birdsong, or gentle rain, can induce a sense of calm and relaxation. Instrumental music, without lyrics, allows the mind to focus on the melodies and harmonies, promoting a meditative and peaceful state.

Personal Preferences: It's worth noting that individual preferences and subjective experiences play a significant role in how different types of music impact the mind. While certain composers or genres may have broad effects on cognition and emotions, the specific response can vary from person to person. Exploring different styles and finding what resonates with you personally is key to optimizing the benefits of music on the mind.

One notable study examining the effects of Baroque music on cognitive function was conducted by Dr. David Stough and his colleagues at Swinburne University in Australia. In their research, they specifically focused on the music of Bach and Vivaldi.

The study involved a group of participants who were divided into three conditions: one group listened to Bach's music, another group listened to Vivaldi's music, and a control group did not listen to any music. The participants' cognitive function was assessed before and after the listening session.

The results of the study revealed several interesting findings. Participants who listened to Bach's music showed improvements in cognitive performance, including enhanced attention and working memory. Similarly, those who listened to Vivaldi's music also demonstrated improvements in cognitive abilities, particularly in attention and processing speed.

The researchers attributed these positive effects to various factors inherent in Baroque music. Baroque compositions often feature intricate melodies, complex harmonies, and precise rhythmic patterns. The combination of these elements is believed to engage the brain in a way that stimulates cognitive processes.

One hypothesis suggests that the complex structure and patterns in Baroque music capture the listener's attention and activate neural networks associated with attentional control. This heightened attention allows for improved focus and concentration, leading to enhanced cognitive performance.

Furthermore, the tempo and rhythm of Baroque music may have a stimulating effect on the brain. Many Baroque compositions, including those by Bach and Vivaldi, feature lively and energetic tempos that can promote a state of alertness and mental arousal. This heightened arousal may contribute to increased cognitive performance.

Another important aspect of Baroque music is its predictable and organized nature. The clear structure and repetitive patterns found in many Baroque compositions provide a sense of order and familiarity. This predictability may create a comforting and soothing effect on the mind, allowing for improved cognitive processing and memory retention.

In addition to the specific findings of this study, research on the effects of classical music, including Baroque compositions, has shown broader benefits for the mind. Listening to classical music has been associated with reduced stress levels, enhanced mood, and increased relaxation. These factors can indirectly contribute to improved cognitive function and mental well-being.

It's important to note that individual responses to music can vary, and the effects of Baroque music on cognitive function may differ from person to person. Factors such as personal preferences, familiarity with the music, and previous experiences can influence the individual's response.

Research suggests that listening to the music of Baroque composers like Johann Sebastian Bach and Antonio Vivaldi can have positive effects on cognitive function. The complex melodies, intricate harmonies, and rhythmic patterns of Baroque music engage the brain and enhance attention, working memory, and other cognitive processes. The predictable structure and soothing nature of Baroque compositions also contribute to a sense of order and relaxation. While the specific mechanisms underlying these effects require further exploration, the study of Baroque music's impact on the mind opens up intriguing possibilities for harnessing the power of music to enhance cognitive abilities and promote mental well-being.

Additional research indicates that a wide range of music genres and composers can have positive effects on the mind and well-being. While the Mozart effect has garnered attention, it is not limited to his music alone. Whether it's the intricate compositions of Baroque masters, the soothing qualities of ambient music, or the timeless classics of various composers, the power of music to influence the mind is a rich and diverse field of study.

Meditation Helps the Mind

Meditation is a practice that has been used for centuries to promote mental well-being and cultivate a sense of inner peace and clarity. Here's a detailed explanation of how meditation helps the mind:

Reduces Stress and Anxiety: One of the primary benefits of meditation is its ability to reduce stress and anxiety. When we meditate, we activate the relaxation response in our bodies, which counteracts the effects of the stress response. Regular meditation practice helps lower levels of stress hormones like cortisol, promoting a calmer state of mind. By training the mind to focus on the present moment, meditation helps alleviate anxious thoughts and cultivates a sense of inner peace.

Enhances Emotional Well-being: Meditation supports emotional well-being by increasing awareness of our emotions and improving our ability to regulate them. Through meditation, we develop a greater sense of self-awareness, allowing us to recognize and acknowledge our emotions without getting caught up in them. This increased awareness helps us respond to emotions in a more skillful and balanced way, promoting emotional resilience and positive emotional states.

Improves Concentration and Focus: Regular meditation practice has been shown to improve concentration and focus. During meditation, we train our minds to stay present and anchored to a specific object of focus, such as the breath or a mantra. This practice strengthens our ability to sustain attention and resist distractions. Over time, meditation enhances our ability to concentrate not only during the practice itself, but also in other aspects of our lives.

Cultivates Mindfulness: Mindfulness is the practice of paying attention to the present moment with openness and non-judgmental awareness. Meditation is a powerful tool for cultivating mindfulness. By directing our attention to the present moment during meditation, we train ourselves to be more mindful in everyday life. This heightened state of awareness allows us to fully engage with our experiences, savoring the positive moments and navigating challenges with greater clarity and equanimity.

Promotes Positive Thinking: Meditation can help cultivate positive thinking patterns by increasing awareness of our thought patterns and their impact on our well-being. As we observe our thoughts during meditation, we become more attuned to the habitual negative or unhelpful thought patterns that may arise. Through regular practice, we can learn to disengage from these patterns and choose more positive and constructive thoughts.

Meditation also helps us develop a compassionate and non-judgmental attitude towards our thoughts, allowing us to cultivate a positive and supportive inner dialogue.

Enhances Self-awareness and Self-compassion: Meditation deepens our understanding of ourselves, fostering self-awareness and self-compassion. Through the practice of non-judgmental observation, we gain insight into our thoughts, emotions, and behaviors. This self-awareness allows us to develop a greater understanding of our strengths, weaknesses, and patterns of behavior. With increased self-awareness, we can make conscious choices that align with our values and well-being. Meditation also cultivates self-compassion, allowing us to treat ourselves with kindness and understanding, even in the face of challenges or self-criticism.

Supports Brain Health: Scientific research has proven that meditation has positive effects on brain structure and function. Regular meditation practice can lead to changes in the brain associated with improved attention, emotional regulation, and memory. It has been found to increase the thickness of the prefrontal cortex, a brain region associated with decision-making and emotional regulation. Additionally, meditation has been linked to reduced activity in the amygdala, the brain's fear center, resulting in decreased reactivity to stress and negative emotions.

Meditation is a powerful practice that benefits the mind in numerous ways. It reduces stress and anxiety, enhances emotional well-being, improves concentration and focus, cultivates mindfulness, promotes positive thinking. You don't have to make a big show of it with candles and music. Occasionally, you can just meditate in your car for five or ten minutes.

Snapping Out of It- Quick Change

1. Take some deep breaths - Inhale slowly through your nose, feel your belly expand with air. Exhale slowly out your mouth. Deep breathing reduces stress and calms the mind.

2. Go for a short walk outside - Fresh air and movement will give you an energizing change of scenery. Observe nature around you.

3. Listen to uplifting music - Choose songs with positive messages or upbeat tempo to lift your spirit. Sing or dance along.

4. Call or text a friend - Connecting with loved ones provides emotional support and reminds you of the good in your life.

5. Watch a funny video - Laughter instantly boosts mood. Search for stand-up comedy or funny animal clips to get giggling.

6. Do light stretches - Shaking out the body helps release stuck energy contributing to bad moods. Stretch your arms overhead and twist side to side.

7. Snack on your favorite healthy treat - Comfort foods that make you smile, provide association to happiness. Keep nutritious snacks on hand.

8. Make a cup of herbal tea - Sip slowly and mindfully. Notice the warmth, aroma, and flavor. Chamomile and lavender teas are calming.

9. Write in a gratitude journal - Shift focus to blessings in your life, however small. Uplifts mood and perspective.

10. Look at photos or videos that make you happy - Reminisce on positive memories of loved ones, fun times, places that brought joy.

11. Give someone a genuine compliment - Doing for others lifts the spirit. Tell them what you admire or appreciate about them.

12. Tidy up clutter - Getting organized reduces overwhelm that can negatively affect mood. Plus, seeing neat spaces is uplifting.

13. Spend time with a pet - Caring for animals and their unconditional affection boosts oxytocin, comforts the heart.

14. Do something creative - Crafting, drawing, coloring, playing an instrument engages your imagination to distract the funk.

15. Get a change of scenery - Visit a beautiful nature spot or somewhere uplifting. Stimulate your senses.

16. Do a random act of kindness - Helping others elevates morale and purpose. Surprise someone by doing a favor.

17. Take a quick shower or bath - Let water wash away stress. Add calming scents to your bath, like lavender or eucalyptus.

18. Declutter your space - Clear out messes that drag energy down. Donate unused items. Organize shelves and drawers.

19. Spend time gardening or with plants - Nurturing plants cultivates joy. Soil's microbial health may balance mood.

20. Call a help line - Speaking with a supportive listener when very down provides relief and hope.

21. Hug a loved one - Physical affection releases oxytocin, easing anxiety. Hug your child, partner, friend, or pet.

22. Dance around - Moving your whole body to music uplifts mood quickly. Crank up an energizing song and boogie.

23. Make a comforting meal - Cooking involves all senses and can be therapeutic. Enjoy comfort foods that nourish body and soul.

24. Watch cute animal videos - Looking at the playful antics of animals stimulates feel-good endorphins and laughter.

25. Practice 10 minutes of meditation - Clearing your mind reduces overthinking that can drag down moods. Simply breathe.

26. Go sit in sunlight outdoors - Sunlight exposure increases serotonin that stabilizes mood. Spend 10–15 minutes in the sunlight.

27. Listen to a guided mindfulness meditation - Soothing voices help you tune into the present moment to de-stress.

28. Take an Epsom salt bath - Magnesium in the salts gets absorbed through skin to relax the body and regulate mood.

29. Do a quick tidy of your home - Get a sense of accomplishment plus uplifted by neater surroundings.

30. Read an inspiring book passage - Uplifting quotes and stories boost positivity, meaning, and encouragement.

31. Stretch gently before bed - Light yoga releases muscle tension so you can rest better. Try child's pose, figure, four stretches.

32. Practice positive self-talk - Counter pessimistic thoughts with affirming statements like "This will pass soon" or "I've got this!"

33. Call a crisis line if extremely distressed - Don't hesitate to get professional support if your mood is dangerous low. You matter.

34. Let yourself cry - Releasing emotions relieves pressure. Crying engages the parasympathetic nervous system to calm you.

35. Focus on solutions, not problems - Reframe issues by asking "How can I improve this?" Action reduces helplessness.

36. Write down what's bothering you - Expressing turmoil on paper brings clarity and releases stuck energy.

37. Take a warm shower or bath - Let the water soothe away your worries. Add Epsom or Himalayan bath salts.

38. Tidy or reorganize your room - Accomplishment plus calming surroundings positively shifts your state.

39. Talk to a counselor or coach - Get constructive feedback to gain new perspectives and action plans.

40. Do gentle stretches - Release muscle tension that accumulates with emotional stress. Try neck rolls, chest openers.

41. Make a point to really taste your food - Eat a small wholesome snack mindfully, savoring flavors.

42. Play with a pet or child - Laughing and delight lifts spirits instantly. Toss a ball, play tug of war, tickle.

43. Listen to nature sounds - Crickets, ocean, rainfall produce instantly soothing ambient noise.

44. Envision your happy place - Imagining a beautiful, serene place activates the parasympathetic nervous system.

45. Do a quick tidy up - Accomplishing small tasks gives you a sense of control over your environment.

46. Say positive affirmations - "I am strong. This will pass. I can handle this." Programs the mind optimistically.

47. Plan an uplifting activity - Having something fun on the calendar cheers you up in the moment and gives you something to look forward to.

48. Help someone else - Get out of your head by doing a favor for someone. Offer support, run an errand, give a gift.

49. Visualize your worries floating away - Picture troubles as clouds passing by or leaves floating down a stream.

50. Follow an online workout video - Movement releases endorphins and tension. Even 10 minutes can energize.

51. Take a quick walk around the block - Moving your body and seeing nature shifts your state. Breathe deep.

52. Read a poem or inspirational quotes - Uplifting words stir optimism. Read Rumi, Mary Oliver, Maya Angelou.

53. Declutter one area - Goal-focused action creates a sense of control. Toss unused items, neatly organize.

54. Listen to a guided imagery meditation - Soothing voices lead you to mentally picture relaxing scenes.

55. Make a cup of warm herbal tea - Sip calming tea like chamomile, lavender, ginger, turmeric, mint.

56. Stretch body gently - Release muscle tension with twists, chest openers. Especially the shoulders and neck.

57. Write a list of things you're grateful for - Reminds you of blessings, goodness in life. Studies show gratitude boosts mood.

58. Let yourself laugh - Watch silly videos. Have a belly laugh. Laughter instantly lightens your load.

59. Pick a small goal and accomplish it - A sense of achievement motivates you to keep taking positive steps.

60. Give someone a hug - Physical affection releases feel-good hormones like oxytocin.

61. Tidy your room - An orderly environment brings a sense of calm and control.

62. Play upbeat energizing music - Sing, dance around to shift your vibe. Crank your favorite song!

63. Take a relaxing bath or shower - Let go of the day's stresses. Add Epsom salts or lavender oil.

64. Take a few moments to breathe deeply - Bring yourself back to the present. Focus on the sensations of inhaling and exhaling.

65. Stretch gently - Release muscle tension, especially in the neck and shoulders, where we store stress. Try spinal twists.

66. Reframe your thoughts - Counter negative thinking with rational responses. "This is only temporary." "I've overcome setbacks before."

67. Treat yourself to something special - A special snack, coffee drink, new book. Remember that you are worth it!

68. Have a good cry - Releasing emotions relieves pressure. Botanical tissue works great for blowing your nose!

69. Take a nap - Getting extra rest recharges your mood and energy. Keep naps 15–20 minutes.

70. Do something you enjoy - Hobbies that engage your creativity or fun lift spirits - cook, paint, play music, knit.

71. Help someone - Distract yourself by doing a favor for someone. Surprise them by offering support.

72. Cuddle a pet or loved one - Physical affection releases oxytocin to comfort and calm. Hug it out!

73. Declutter space - External order brings internal calm. Toss unused items, organize shelves and drawers.

74. Listen to a funny podcast - Laughter instantly lightens your perspective and mood.

75. Dance to a favorite upbeat song - Freestyle dancing gets your endorphins pumping. Shake it off!

76. Practice positive self-talk - Remind yourself of strengths, past successes, reasons for optimism about the future.

77. Make a comfort meal - Cooking engages senses to soothe. Enjoy healthy comforting foods.

78. Change your environment - Step outside, visit a pretty nature spot, go to a friend's house. New scenery shifts mood.

79. Call a friend - Talking helps release worries and reconnects you to support. Laughter with loved one's uplifts.

80. Exercise - Take a brisk walk, do yoga, lift weights. Working out alleviates depression.

81. Practice deep breathing - Inhale deeply through your nose, exhale slowly through your mouth. Calms mind and body.

82. Be present - Slow down and focus your senses on the visual details around you. Getting out of your head lightens the mood.

83. Help someone in need - Get out by doing a favor for someone else. Be a good listener, run an errand.

84. Get outdoors - Fresh air, sunlight, and nature nourish our spirits. Take your shoes off, walk on the grass.

85. Stargaze - Looking at the night sky puts your problems in perspective. You are part of a vast, beautiful universe!

86. Take an Epsom salt bath - Magnesium absorbs through skin, reducing inflammation that can lower mood. Add lavender oil too.

87. Chat with positive friends - Surround yourself with uplifting people who encourage rather than pull you down.

88. Watch cute animal videos - Funny kittens or babies giggling make instant mood boosters!

89. Use adaptogen herbs - Ashwagandha, Rhodiola Rosea, Holy Basil (Tulsi) to alleviate anxiety and depression.

90. Make a fun plan - Having something to look forward to gives you motivation now. Schedule a movie night, hiking trip, or dinner with friends.

91. Clean and organize your space - An orderly environment creates a sense of control that calms your mind.

92. Write in a journal - Expressing your feelings brings clarity and relief. Write a list of things you're grateful for.

93. Take a magnesium supplement - Magnesium calms the nervous system and muscles. Capsules, calm drink mixes, Epsom salt baths.

94. Laugh aloud - Make silly faces in the mirror, watch a comedy show, laugh for no reason! Laughter instantly uplifts.

95. Plan a trip - Researching future adventures gives you motivation now to work through current sadness and look forward to joy!

96. Lift weights - Strength training releases endorphins and tension. Feel stronger physically and emotionally.

97. Declutter - Choose one area like a drawer or shelf to tidy up. You'll feel a sense of control and calm.

98. Do a random act of kindness - Helping someone lifts your spirits and takes the focus off your worries!

99. Take a magnesium supplement - Magnesium helps regulate mood, reduces anxiety and aids sleep.

100. Get a change of scenery - Visit somewhere beautiful or uplifting like a nature trail, museum, uplifting friend's house.

101. Spend time with or hugging an animal - Our furry friends comfort us and brighten our day. Take your dog for a walk or pet the cat.

102. Watch an inspiring movie or video - Uplifting stories boost motivation and mood. Documentaries can provide perspective.

103. Clean up your environment - Having an orderly living space brings a sense of calm and accomplishment.

104. Take a nap - Rest and restore your perspective. Keep naps 10-20 minutes to avoid grogginess.

105. Make a comforting meal - Cooking can be therapeutic, plus comfort foods make you smile.

106. Stretch your body - Release muscle tension that builds up with emotional stress. Try chest openers, neck rolls.

107. Compliment others - Recognizing the good in others lifts your spirits. Write a nice note to someone.

108. Improve your posture - Sit up straight, roll back your shoulders. Posture affects mood and confidence.

109. Take a break from news and social media - Getting perspective from unplugging helps reduce anxiety.

110. Plan something rewarding for the end of the day - Give yourself a light at the end of the tunnel - relaxing bath, favorite show, comfortable pajamas.

111. Listen to an uplifting podcast - Hear stories of perseverance, recovery, thriving through difficulties to gain perspective.

112. Be around positive people - Attitudes are contagious! Avoid those who feed your funk. Surround yourself with optimism.

113. Walk in nature - Moving your body outdoors nourishes your spirit. Breathe fresh air, soak up the healing sunlight.

114. Make a cozy space - Light candles, wrap yourself in a soft blanket, create hygge. Comfort calms the mind.

115. Declutter your closet - Donating unused items clears energy and brings a sense of renewal. Clear space, clear mind!

116. Watch the sunrise - New days bring fresh starts and possibilities. Embrace the gift of being alive at this moment.

117. Organize your space - Outer order brings inner calm. A tidy room reduces overwhelm that depresses moods.

118. Give yourself permission to feel it - Sadness must be felt before it can pass. Cry if you need to, then focus on lifting yourself back up.

119. Take a nature walk - Soaking in the sights, sounds and smells of nature soothes the soul. Try forest bathing.

120. Make a cozy space - Light candles, wrap yourself in a blanket, create hygge. Soothing surroundings comfort the mind.

121. Watch funny animal videos - Smile and laugh! Playful, silly animals are instant joy boosters.

122. Try aromatherapy - Uplifting essential oils like grapefruit, lavender, orange can influence mood. Add to bath or diffuser.

123. Get a change of environment - Visit somewhere beautiful or meaningful - a nature trail, meaningful building. New sights stimulate.

124. Take a magnesium supplement - Magnesium helps regulate mood and aids sleep. Capsules, bath flakes, calm drink mixes.

125. Find a reason to laugh - Play with a pet or child. Watch bloopers or funny home videos. Laughter instantly uplifts.

126. Take a brisk walk - Moving your body releases feel-good endorphins, plus you get outdoors into nature.

127. Cook or bake something comforting - Cooking engages your senses. Enjoy cozy, nourishing foods.

128. Give hugs - Holding loved ones close releases bonding oxytocin. Give the gift of a hug today.

129. Buy yourself flowers - Surrounding yourself with natural beauty brings instant joy.

130. Positive music - Create a playlist of songs with upbeat tempo and inspiring lyrics to shift your mood fast.

131. Fix up your space - Declutter messes that drag you down. Wipe counters, take out trash, tidy up.

132. Reframe your thoughts - Catch negative talk and consciously shift perspective. "I can do hard things." "This will pass."

133. Connect with supportive people - Talk or text a positive friend or family member. Make plans to meet.

134. Be gentle with yourself - Treat yourself as you would a good friend in need. Be patient and compassionate.

135. Do a quick home tidy - Restore order to your environment so it feels calmer and more organized.

136. Stretch gently - Simple stretches can release tension, especially in the neck, shoulders and back.

137. Take a power nap - 10 to 20 minutes of daytime sleep reboots your system so you awaken refreshed.

138. Declutter countertops - Clear surfaces of clutter that piles up and drags on your mood. Toss junk, neatly organize.

139. Watch funny videos - Laughter immediately boosts your mood! Belly laugh at funny clips on YouTube.

140. Diffuse essential oils - Uplifting scents like grapefruit, lemon, peppermint can influence emotions.

141. Let go of what you can't control - Make peace with the current moment and trust things will improve soon.

142. Straighten your posture - Stand tall, pull shoulders back. Posture affects confidence and mood.

143. Write down your feelings - Getting worries out on paper releases them from your mind. Vent on paper!

144. Dance it out! Turn on upbeat music and dance like no one's watching! Shake it off.

145. Take care of a plant - Nurturing new life is therapeutic. Watering and tending to a plant cheers you up.

146. Make a gratitude list - Shifts focus to blessings in your life, however small. Count your gifts.

147. Visualize your happy place - Imagine somewhere beautiful and serene that calms your mind and heart.

That Little Inner Voice That is Always Talking to Us

Training the inner voice to feed more positive thoughts throughout the day:

Our inner voice plays a powerful role in shaping our moment-to-moment experiences. Often referred to as our "self-talk", this voice can uplift or undermine us with its running commentary. With conscious effort, we can reframe negative self-talk into a supportive inner ally.

The first step is increasing awareness of your inner voice's tendencies. Notice when your self-talk becomes critical, pessimistic, worrisome or defeatist. Catch yourself mid-thought. Simply observing rather than engaging these narratives begins to diffuse their power over you.

When you tune into your inner voice, identify specifically the types of negative thoughts arising - "There's my inner critic attacking my abilities again" or "I'm worried about the future again." Name the patterns happening in the moment rather than believing the thoughts or judging yourself.

Rather than resist or suppress negative self-talk, approach it with curiosity and compassion. This inner voice is just a conditioned set of thoughts and beliefs, not your true essence. Thank your mind for trying to protect you from perceived threats. Then gently guide it in more uplifting directions.

Reflect on the emotions generated when your inner voice becomes negative anger, sadness, fear, shame. Your self-talk influences how you feel. Consider if this voice is serving your wellbeing or undermining it. Does it lift you up or drag you down?

When you notice unhelpful self-talk, pause and interrupt the pattern. Say "stop" silently to yourself. Breathe deeply. This creates space between stimulus and response, empowers you to respond consciously.

Ask yourself if the inner narrative is entirely true and realistic by looking objectively at the evidence. Is the voice exaggerating or panicking? Talk to yourself like you would a dear friend, with kindness.

Rather than argue with negative thoughts, practice reframing them. How else could you view the situation that would be more helpful? Even difficult circumstances contain opportunities to learn and grow if you shift perspective.

Replace harsh self-criticisms with compassion. Talk to yourself as you would a loved one struggling. Ask, "What do I most need to hear right now to feel supported? What would be helpful, rather than harmful?"

Affirm your inherent strengths, abilities, worthiness, and capacity to handle challenges. This builds self-trust. Remind yourself, "I've overcome difficult times before, I can do this too."

When inner talk drifts to past regret, gently guide your mind back into the present moment. The past cannot be changed, but you have the power to create a beautiful future by your actions now.

Spend time visualizing desired outcomes you would like to manifest - improved relationships, career accomplishments, better health. Instruct your mind to generate thoughts that align with your goals.

Challenge extreme all-or-nothing thinking. Ask yourself, "Is there another way I could view this situation that's more balanced and realistic?" Cultivate nuance.

Notice when fear-based thoughts arise about the future. Bring yourself back into the present, where you are actually safe and okay. Breathe, relax your body, look around.

Separate your sense of self-worth from external validation. You are inherently worthy simply because you exist, not because of what you achieve. Let this truth sink in.

Consciously start narrating your day from an optimistic, appreciative lens. Find the positive in each experience. Be on the lookout for blessings.

Minimize time spent with sources that breed negative thinking, like certain social media, news, or people. Nourish your mind with positivity.

Start your mornings by setting an intention to be mindful of your thoughts and receptive to inner positivity throughout the day.

Keep a gratitude journal where you write down feelings of thankfulness and contentment. This reminds you of the ongoing good.

Make a list of small joys and pleasures you can easily access when you need a quick positivity boost - favorite teas, cozy blankets, upbeat songs.

Set alerts on your phone reminding you to check in with yourself at regular intervals. Ask, "Is my self-talk currently life-giving?" Then adjust accordingly.

Surround yourself with positive influences like hopeful friends, inspiring media, elevating environments. Their energy rubs off on you.

Have trusting listeners in your life you can turn to when you are unable to stop spiraling into heavy self-talk. They can uplift you.

Try repeating an empowering mantra that affirms your strengths. "I am grounded. I am loved. I am enough." Mantras break negative thought loops.

Write down empowering messages and place them around your home or office as uplifting reminders - on mirrors, walls, desks.

Wear or carry an object like a bracelet or stone in your pocket that symbolizes hope, strength, protection. Touch it when needing reassurance.

Make a playlist of positive songs with encouraging lyrics to immerse your mind in uplifting messages and energy.

Set goals to cultivate positive personal qualities like patience, wisdom, courage, compassion. Aligning actions with values builds self-esteem.

Practice mindfulness meditation to strengthen awareness of your inner voice without identifying with or judging its narratives. Be the observer.

If troubling thoughts arise while trying to sleep, keep a journal by your bed to write them down so they're released from your head.

Welcome emotions without exaggerating their importance or meaning. "I feel sad right now. This too shall pass." Don't let them define you.

See personal setbacks as feedback, not as proof of inadequacy. Adapt, grow wiser, evolve. Maintain perspective.

When you catch your inner voice being negative, inject some humor. Imagine silly ways you could alter the dialogue to be ridiculous.

Most importantly, be patient and forgiving with yourself as you learn to transform self-talk patterns. Old habits take time to rewire. Notice progress.

With consistent practice, you can retrain your inner voice to be an unconditional ally that nurtures your growth, heals wounds, and guides you gracefully through life's joys and challenges.

Powering Down the Mind is Actually a Great Thing to Do

Our busy modern lives often leave little time for contemplation. We rush through days packed with obligations, constantly stimulated and reacting, with little pause to process experiences. However, reflecting and thinking are vital human needs for maintaining a peaceful mind. Setting aside downtime lets thoughts settle so we can return to activities refreshed and centered.

Allowing your mind time to wander without an agenda permits new connections to form from existing ideas. This kind of nonlinear thinking sparks creativity and problem-solving. Solutions arise seemingly spontaneously when we disengage from intentional thought. Without time for reflection, we lack opportunities for insights to crystalize.

Pausing also helps provide clarity amidst chaos. When demands pile endlessly upon each other, it's easy to feel scattered and overwhelmed. Regularly taking breaks to think - even for 5–10 minutes - creates space between tasks so they don't blur together. You regain perspective on priorities when granted mental breathing room.

Downtime also allows you to consciously process emotions and experiences rather than reacting reflexively. Pressures often compel us to keep pushing ahead without digesting the meaning of events. Self-reflection helps you integrate lessons so they don't keep resurfacing later as unresolved tensions.

Without the distraction of constant activity, your mind can wander to profound existential questions about your purpose, relationships, values, and direction in life. Downtime lets you contemplate who you are at your core - your needs, passions, and goals. Periodically gazing inward is part of meaningful living.

Being comfortable with solitude takes the edge off loneliness. Too much busyness can mask emptiness inside. Regular alone time teaches you your own company is enough, since you're at home with your thoughts. Your sense of peace comes from within.

Mindfully occupying yourself also builds patience, contentment, and self-sufficiency. You discover small pleasures in ordinary moments without depending on external stimulation. You realize you already possess so much.

In relaxed downtime, you're able to consider your thoughts and feelings with compassionate detachment, rather than harsh self-judgment. Getting distance from your inner chatter allows you to respond thoughtfully, rather than reactively.

Without the pressure to produce something, you can simply explore ideas playfully. Let concepts incubate and synthesize. Time-stamping every action robs the imagination of space and freedom. There should be room for whimsy.

Downtime replenishes mental resources that pouring nonstop effort gradually depletes over weeks and months. Time off fills your cup so you can keep giving your best. Periodic recharging preserves passion for your work and relationships.

Finally, with no rush toward the next obligation, you can fully soak in the joys of ordinary moments - listening to music, staring out a window, sipping tea. Life's beauty often hides in plain sight, revealed only when you pause to appreciate it.

In our productivity-driven world, scheduling downtime can seem counterintuitive or even indulgent. But human beings aren't machines. We require untethered time to integrate experiences into wisdom. Find pockets each day to unplug and reflect - to know yourself and drink from life's wellspring. Keep tending your inner garden.

We Never Quit

WHY we should never quit and how quitting small things can lead to bigger issues down the road:

Life inevitably brings challenges, hardship, and stress. When faced with difficulties, it's tempting to want to quit - to walk away from responsibilities, abandon goals or give up on dreams. Taking the easy way out can seem appealing in the moment, but quitting often makes situations worse in the long run. Building the habit of perseverance, even when quitting seems justified, leads to greater success and satisfaction in life.

Quitting Can Become a Habit

Human nature loves comfort. We want to avoid unpleasantness. Quitting something difficult provides short-term relief. But quick fixes come at a cost. Each time we quit, it becomes a bit easier to do so again. We reinforce the neural pathways in our brain associated with giving up, making it more likely we'll quit next time adversity strikes. Success in any endeavor requires discipline and grit. Quitting damages those mental "muscles", making it harder to stick with anything challenging. Like a snowball effect, quitting small things leads to justifying quitting bigger ones down the road.

The pull to take the easy way out never disappears. To achieve major goals like finishing school, building a business or raising a family requires persevering through ongoing discomfort. If you condition yourself to quit when faced with normal obstacles, you'll likely falter at the first sign of struggle on important ventures. Regularly quitting small commitments chips away at the mental fortitude needed to achieve greater ambitions.

Withdrawing effort prompts regret and disappointment. Unfinished business leaves loose ends we must contend with. Failed responsibilities often come back around to create bigger headaches later. The temporary relief of quitting is quickly replaced by demoralization and lower self-esteem. In contrast, seeing commitments through to completion builds pride and self-confidence. Developing a habit of persistence leads to earning bigger and bigger wins, fueling motivation.

Quitting Can Start a Downward Spiral

Quitting one responsibility frequently leads to a cascade effect. Maybe you drop a club you joined, which causes disappointment and hurt feelings in others counting on you. Their reaction prompts you to withdraw from more social commitments. Minor friendships fade, leaving you more isolated. Laziness sets in, so you skip workouts. Soon, your fitness slides, along with your mood and motivation. Quarrels arise with your romantic partner, but instead of working through issues, you break up. What started as quitting a small obligation turned into a major downward life spiral.

Often what we quit are positive habits and endeavors improving life, if only we could push through the initial discomfort. Whether it's exercise, acquiring new skills, building relationships or advancing a career, progress requires patience. A little short-term pain earns substantial long-term gain. Quitting may temporarily ease pain, but sacrificing opportunities for growth keeps you stuck. Each time you quit something beneficial, you slide a bit further downwards.

Bouncing back becomes harder once you have gathered momentum going the wrong direction. Turning it around demands making difficult changes. The longer you live with the consequences of quitting important endeavors, the deeper the hole you dig for yourself. It takes tremendous effort to halt a downward trajectory and point yourself back upwards. Far better to cultivate tenacity and avoid this fate to begin with.

Quitting Can Close Off Future Opportunities

Most regrets come from paths not taken. Each juncture in life offers possibilities. Taking the easy way out by quitting often closes alternative routes. Turning down an invitation today may mean you don't get invited tomorrow. Bailing on a networking coffee meet forfeits building useful contacts. Abandoning the chance to gain new skills leaves you unqualified for better jobs. The opportunity cost of quitting is invisible, but very real.

Years later, you never know what might have developed from something you quit prematurely. Maybe that dance class you dropped out of would have introduced you to your future spouse. Perhaps the book you abandoned halfway through would have sparked a passion leading to a deeply fulfilling career. We cannot recognize roads not traveled. But looking back, we often lament quitting endeavors that may have completely altered our lives for the better.

Quitting Provides Temporary Relief, But Resolves Nothing

Quitting usually feels like an escape from discomfort. The temptation is to believe removing yourself will make problems disappear. In reality, challenges rarely vanish on their own. Lingering issues continue plaguing you or pop up elsewhere. Quitting just delays finding an actual resolution.

Whether it's a frustrating job, a faltering relationship or overwhelming debts, the answer lies in methodically taking steps to improve the situation. While incredibly difficult, confronting concerns head on builds skills, knowledge, and wisdom you can apply to other aspects of life. Quitting prevents cultivating strengths needed to overcome adversity. Any relief proves all too brief before related troubles arise.

True growth comes from leaning into difficulties and learning to adapt. Physically quitting something does not make internal turmoil disappear. Reconciling yourself mentally and emotionally to challenges requires digging deeper, not turning away. By sticking through tough times, you better understand yourself and how to create the life you want. Quitting wastes opportunities to develop wisdom gained no other way.

Perseverance Builds Inner Strength

Strength of character shows itself not when things go smoothly, but in response to troubles. Rocky terrain prompts roots to grow deeper. Similarly, facing trials reinforces our mental "roots" if we do not give up. Withstanding difficulties builds grit, maturity, and self-knowledge. Emerging through hardships equips us to handle future obstacles.

Visualize challenges as weight being added to a barbell. Taking the easy way out by dropping the weight altogether forfeits the strength developed by lifting it. But persevering straining to build metaphorical muscles. Gradually, what once seemed impossible becomes manageable. Intensity that used to crush you now feels within your power.

While quick escapes are tempting, ultimately shallow, there are no shortcuts to depth of character. What we get out depends on what we put in. Through long journeys, we become our best selves. The only failures are giving up or refusing to begin. If you fall down seven times, get up eight. Persistence through trying times unlocks rewards that ease cannot.

When Progress Seems Halted, Assess and Adjust

Every so often we hit plateaus where persevering as usual yields no results. Old strategies may have exhausted their usefulness. Instead of quitting entirely when forward momentum ceases, pause and reflect.

Ask sincere questions about what is not working and how circumstances could shift. Maybe you need a new approach, different resources or outside help. Perhaps resting and recovering mentally prepares you to keep pushing. Evolve your thinking to match new realities.

Experiment and get creative about adjusting tactics. Switch mediums, find another venue, or talk to someone else encountering similar struggles. Try coming at the issue sideways instead of head on. Risk unorthodox methods outside your comfort zone. Be willing to make major changes, not just minor tweaks.

Progress rarely follows a straight line. Setbacks and standstills are natural phases in an upward winding journey. Minimize unnecessary backsliding by adapting smartly when movement stalls. As long as you do not fully quit, you retain the possibility of finding your way through. Trust that growth awaits on the other side of disillusionment.

Help Others Who Struggle Against Quitting

Urging others to persevere multiplies benefits beyond just encouraging them. By reminding someone else why they should not quit their passion project, marriage or sobriety, you reinforce those principles within yourself. The empathy and care shown toward another person's tribulations builds your compassion and resolve.

When you see someone struggling where you once did, your experience makes you uniquely qualified to help them through it. You understand their frustrations and temptations to quit in an in-depth way. Sharing hard-won wisdom boosts their morale and renews your purpose.

There is no stronger invitation to pursue excellence than someone in need. Their potential depends in part on the support you offer. To fulfill obligations to them, you rededicate yourself to your perseverance. Together, you make each other stronger. Wherever someone else is ready to quit, you now have an opportunity to make a difference by inspiring them onward.

In summary, while quitting temporarily eases pain, it often exacerbates problems. Cultivating perseverance in small matters fortifies the grit required for major goals. Progress requires pushing through plateaus, not giving up. Shared hardship overcome builds powerful communal bonds. Hard-won wisdom justifies difficult paths taken. The only unacceptable choice is to stand still. Character and opportunity grow through ceaseless self-improvement, no matter the obstacles faced along the way.

Recharging the Brain

The Ultimate Brain Recharge, the nap. But Does it Help?

I have been a Giant supporter of the nap. In my Youth I would go from work, to class, to the gym to a softball game all with just a 15-minute nap under the trees in the car before the game. It worked for me, and still does. What do the experts say?

Taking a nap is not only a delightful indulgence, but also a scientifically proven way to recharge your brain and rejuvenate your nervous system. The benefits of napping extend beyond mere relaxation, as they have a profound impact on your cognitive abilities, emotional well-being, and overall brain health. In this article, we will delve into the ways in which a nap can recharge your brain and nervous system and promote relaxation.

The human brain is a remarkable organ that regulates our thoughts, emotions, and actions. However, its functioning can be compromised when we experience fatigue and sleep deprivation. Lack of adequate rest can lead to cognitive impairment, decreased attention span, reduced problem-solving abilities, and even negative mood states. Napping provides an opportunity for the brain to recover from these detrimental effects.

When you take a nap, your brain transitions through different stages of sleep, including non-rapid eye movement (NREM) sleep and rapid eye movement (REM) sleep. NREM sleep consists of several stages, with the deepest stage known as slow-wave sleep. This stage is crucial for the restoration of the body and mind. During slow-wave sleep, the brain repairs and regenerates cells, consolidates memories, and clears out unnecessary information, allowing for optimal cognitive functioning.

Napping has been shown to enhance memory and learning processes. During a nap, the brain consolidates new information and forms connections between different pieces of knowledge. This consolidation process leads to improved memory recall and enhances the ability to retain and process information. In fact, research has demonstrated that individuals who nap after learning to perform better on memory tests compared to those who do not nap.

Furthermore, a nap can boost creativity and problem-solving abilities. When you are sleep-deprived, your ability to think creatively and find innovative solutions to challenges may be compromised. By taking a nap, you give your brain the opportunity to process complex information and make novel connections, leading to enhanced creative thinking.

In addition to cognitive benefits, napping plays a crucial role in emotional well-being. When you are tired, emotions can become more intense, and it may be challenging to regulate them effectively. Taking a nap can help regulate emotions by reducing stress and promoting relaxation. During sleep, the brain releases hormones and neurotransmitters that contribute to a sense of calmness and tranquility, helping to alleviate stress and anxiety.

Napping has a positive impact on mood regulation. Lack of sleep has been linked to an increased risk of developing mood disorders such as depression and anxiety. By taking a nap and allowing your brain to rest, you can reset your emotional state, improve your mood, and increase your resilience to stressors. This can lead to a more positive outlook on life and a greater ability to handle daily challenges.

The relaxation induced by a nap also extends to the nervous system. When you are awake, your nervous system is constantly engaged, responding to external stimuli and maintaining various bodily functions. This continuous activity can result in stress and tension. However, when you take a nap, the nervous system can enter a state of rest and recuperation. This allows for the release of built-up tension, a reduction in muscle activity, and a decrease in heart rate and blood pressure.

A nap can have a significant impact on the release of stress hormones. When you are sleep-deprived, the body produces higher levels of stress hormones such as cortisol. These hormones contribute to feelings of anxiety, irritability, and impaired cognitive function. By taking a nap, you can help regulate the levels of stress hormones in your body, leading to a more balanced and relaxed state.

Napping can enhance overall brain health and longevity. Chronic sleep deprivation has been associated with an increased risk of neurodegenerative diseases such as Alzheimer's and Parkinson's. By prioritizing regular naps, you provide your brain with the necessary time to restore and repair itself, reducing the risk of cognitive decline later in life.

What the body goes through when we nap?

Taking a nap is one of the best ways to recharge during the day. Even a short 20-30 minute nap can leave you feeling refreshed and more focused. Here's an overview of what happens in your body when you take a nap:

Sleep Stages

When you first fall asleep during a nap, you go through the early, light stages of non-REM (NREM) sleep. As your body relaxes, your brain waves start to slow down from their waking beta waves into alpha and theta waves. During these stages, you may experience hypnic jerks or have dream-like images flash through your mind even though you aren't in REM sleep yet.

After about 30 minutes, you reach deeper NREM sleep. This is restorative slow-wave sleep where your body and mind can recharge. Your blood pressure and heart rate decrease, breathing slows, muscles relax, and blood supply increases to your muscles to repair themselves. Growth and stress hormones are also released to promote healing.

REM Sleep

If you take a longer nap of 60–90 minutes, you may reach REM (rapid eye movement) sleep, which is when dreams occur. During REM, your eyes move quickly, your breathing becomes irregular, and your heart rate and blood pressure increase closer to waking levels. REM helps consolidate memories and learnings from the day. However, you may feel groggy after waking up from a REM cycle.

The Sleep Cycle

Ideally, you want to wake up at the end of a sleep cycle so you don't feel disoriented. Sleep cycles last about 90 minutes as you progress from light to deep sleep, then back to REM. Waking in the middle can leave you sleepy and foggy. To improve how you feel after a nap, set an alarm for 20, 45, or 90 minute increments.

Other Nap Benefits

In addition to resting your mind, naps also provide other benefits to your body:

- Improves cognitive function and memory recall

- Reduces stress and anxiety

- Supports your immune system by increasing infection-fighting proteins

- Lowers risk of heart disease by decreasing inflammation and blood pressure

- Helps regulate blood sugar and metabolism to control diabetes

- Boosts mood and fights depression due to serotonin production

Nap Tips

To make the most of your nap time, follow these tips:

- Take naps in the early mid-afternoon when your energy naturally dips

- Limit naps to 20–30 minutes to avoid grogginess

- Find a quiet, dark place with few distractions

- Use soft sounds or music to help induce sleep

- Make napping a regular habit if possible

- Avoid caffeine, nicotine, alcohol and heavy foods before napping

- Wake up slowly and give yourself time to transition

In summary, napping provides a burst of renewal for your mind and body. A short nap can improve your mood, focus, health and overall wellbeing. Understanding the sleep stages and cycles helps optimize napping so you reap the full benefits.

8

Making Lasting Change

How This Book Can Help Others Change Their Lives in a Short Time

The book "I Can, I Will, I Must," explores how to transform your mindset and life through the power of positive thinking. Within its pages, you'll learn techniques to overcome challenges and thrive in the face of adversity. By committing to personal growth and intentionally developing positivity, you can shift any area of your life.

The brain's incredible neuroplasticity enables reshaping of neural pathways. Like a muscle, positive thinking strengthens with exercise. Begin noticing negative self-talk, then consciously reframe it. When you catch "I can't" thoughts, replace them with empowering mantras like "I can", "I will", "I must." Repeating upbeat messages rewires your mind over time. The book provides exercises to make positive thinking a habit.

"I Can, I Will, I Must," emphasizes facing fears that hold you back. Avoidance prolongs suffering, while acknowledging anxieties diminishes their control. Start small, leaning into manageable fears to build emotional resilience. With each uncertainty faced, you gather courage to tackle greater challenges. Anxiety loses its grip through your willingness to persist despite it.

The book also highlights visualization techniques to manifest desired outcomes. Mentally rehearsing goals in vivid detail trains your subconscious to make them reality. Athletes commonly use visualization in this way. Apply it in your life by picturing yourself achieving aims. Your mind believes imaginary experiences, priming you for success.

"I Can, I Will, I Must," recognizes setbacks are inevitable. What matters most is how you respond. View difficulties as necessary steps on a longer journey. Ask, "What lesson does this challenge hold?" Integrate insights as you keep striving forward. Stay present; the past can't limit someone focused on their next step. Progress flows from balanced optimism, not perfectionism.

The author shares his health battles as examples of applying positive thinking during hardship. Despite numerous medical traumas, he reframed each one as temporary detours rather than tragedies. During surgeries, he visualized a happy, active life post-recovery. Meeting struggles with hope allowed him to grow through them. If he found light amidst those depths, you can illuminate any darkness.

Wherever you tell yourself "I can't", "I Can, I Will, I Must," urges you to proclaim, "I can!" Hard times will arise, but your response determines experience. Control your inner world by rejecting disempowering narratives. Positivity lets light into darkness. Strengthening your mindset allows conquering any adversity. You need not remain its passive victim. Transform your life by seizing control of your mind!

Commit to growth and watch obstacles become opportunities. Shift outlook from "I can't" to "I can!" Replace fear with courage through persistence. Visualize the future you want. Release the past's hold. Believe in your resilience and power to change your mind. The book provides practical techniques and inspiration to use your mind for good. Read "I Can, I Will, I Must," to uplift your thinking and live your best life!

Additional Tools to assist your thought change

Affirmation cards - Having a deck of affirmation cards that you can flip through whenever you require a positivity boost is highly effective. Choose cards with short uplifting phrases like "I am worthy",

"I am strong", "I believe in myself". Keep these cards in places you frequent like your bedroom, office, car. When you're feeling stressed or defeated, pull out a card, read the affirmation aloud slowly three times, and let the positive message sink in. Hearing yourself say empowering words will gradually reprogram your self-talk.

Vision boards - Dedicate an hour to going through magazines and cutting out any images that represent your dreams and goals - pictures of exotic travel destinations, a large home, a diploma, or award related to your career ambitions. Arrange the images in a way that is aesthetically pleasing on a cardboard canvas or poster board. Place your finished vision board in your office, above your bed, or somewhere it will catch your eye daily. Seeing visual representations of your goals will keep you focused on positive possibilities rather than dwelling on problems.

Gratitude journal - Carve out five minutes each morning to write down three things you are grateful for in a notebook or journal. They can be relatively small, like enjoying a peaceful cup of coffee, having a reliable car, or getting a good night's sleep. The practice of articulating the positive details trains your brain over time to focus more on what you have rather than what you lack. Gratitude fuels optimism.

Positive music - Make playlists in your preferred music app filled with songs that inspire and uplift you. Look for tunes with energizing beats and empowering lyrics. Listen to these playlists during your commute, while working out, or anytime you need a positivity boost. Research shows upbeat music improves mood, boosts motivation, and combats negative thinking.

Nature time - Plan to spend an hour connecting with nature at least 3 times per week. Escape to a park, hiking trail, beach, or anywhere you have access to greenery and sunlight. As you walk slowly, engage all your senses - notice the calming sounds of birds chirping, breathe in the refreshing natural scents, reach out and touch the textures of leaves and bark. Soaking in the beauty of the natural world lifts your spirit and provides a mental reset.

Exercise - Carve out 30 minutes 4 times per week for heart-pumping physical activity like brisk walking, jogging, cycling, or an aerobics class. Moving your body releases those feel-good endorphins while simultaneously relieving stress and anxiety. You'll finish your workout in a more positive headspace.

Support groups - Seek a local or online meetup group focused on personal growth, motivation, mindfulness, or other uplifting topics. Surrounding yourself with encouraging people who share your commitment to self-improvement will nourish and sustain your positivity. Their energy and mindset will rub off on you.

Therapy - If negative thought patterns feel truly entrenched, work with a licensed therapist who specializes in cognitive behavioral therapy techniques. They can help you identify warped thinking, get to the root of negativity, and implement exercises to change those thought patterns over time. Investing in your mental health takes courage, but yields huge positivity dividends.

Affirmations - Upon waking, choose a simple uplifting phrase like "I am worthy". Repeat it aloud or silently to yourself five times. Likewise, before bed, repeat "I am at peace" five times. Bookending your day with positive affirmations will gradually reprogram your self-beliefs at a subconscious level.

Visualization - Sit in a quiet space, close your eyes, and imagine yourself accomplishing your biggest goal. Envision as many details as possible - what you see, hear, feel when your dream becomes reality. This mental rehearsal primes your mind for positive action. Do this for 5–10 minutes daily.

Positive books - Reading uplifting content imprints positive thoughts and perspectives into your mind. Make it a habit to read biographies of inspirational figures who overcame challenges. Their stories of grit and perseverance in the face of adversity will motivate you to stay positive in your life.

Aromatherapy - Diffuse a few drops of lemon essential oil at home or work to naturally boost mood. The vibrant, uplifting lemon scent stimulates productivity and creativity while reducing stress. Just inhaling the invigorating fragrance will lift your spirits.

Yoga - Take a beginner level yoga class that incorporates breathing exercises, gentle poses, and meditation. The practice calms the mind, reduces anxiety and negative thinking, and helps you become more present focused. Do yoga 2-3 times per week for maximum mood benefits.

Smile - Even forcing a smile when you don't feel like it can shift your mood. The physical act of smiling releases neurotransmitters like dopamine and serotonin that relieve stress. Smile widely for 20 seconds, several times throughout your day.

Willing Yourself Into a Positive Frame of Mind, Sometimes It's Not Immediate

The ability to shift your mindset to a more positive state even in dire circumstances requires tremendous inner strength and self-awareness. When facing adversity, it can be incredibly challenging to override feelings of despair, anxiety, or depression. However, cultivating optimism and hope in the face of hardship is possible with intentional effort and can provide long-term resilience.

The first step is acknowledging the validity of the negative emotions you are experiencing, while also actively choosing to focus your mind on possibility rather than catastrophe. This begins the process of self-generated cognitive reappraisal. Rather than being at the mercy of despair, you become an agent in redirecting your thoughts and interpretations of events toward something more constructive.

With practice, you can learn to interrupt downward emotional spirals and make the conscious choice to view the situation through a lens of opportunity rather than defeat. This could involve reminding yourself of past examples where things worked out in unexpected ways. Envisioning how you might tell the story in the future if the outcome ends up being positive, or looking for any small sign, however minor, that a given situation is not utterly hopeless.

Generating optimism requires flexibility of thought and the discipline to catch yourself when you are making blanket negative assumptions. It means realizing when you have fallen into catastrophizing and making the effort to consider more uplifting perspectives, even if you cannot feel their emotional effect yet.

Additionally, focusing on what is within your control, rather than ruminating on all the external factors you cannot change, is key to willing yourself to a more positive emotional place. You may not be able to determine when the adversity or suffering will end, but you can control your daily thoughts, choices of activity, and the way you treat others around you. Determining one small action you can take today - whether it be an act of self-care, outreach to a friend in need, or working toward a tiny goal - can empower you and be the start of generating hopefulness from within.

However, despite your best conscious efforts to shift your emotional state, you may find that your mood remains despairing rather than instantly transforming. It is crucial to be extremely compassionate with yourself in these circumstances. Recognize that neuronal pathways in your brain have become highly sensitized to stress, uncertainty, and fear. Lifelong neural wiring does not change overnight. The fact your intentional efforts to view the situation more positively do not quickly provide emotional relief does not mean those efforts are in vain.

Be proud that you are making continual choices to at least try to direct your mind away from catastrophic thinking, even if your emotions lag. Over time and with repetition, consciously overriding the negative thought patterns and choosing to seek possibility and sources of hope will start to become more automatic. The neural pathways that reinforce optimism will strengthen.

Additionally, focusing on cultivating positive emotions, even if fleeting, is essential to broaden your outlook. Try to find small moments to sincerely laugh, experience appreciation or awe, or feel gratitude even amid adversity. Generate positive emotion through music, poetry, observing nature, or meditation. This builds your capacity to experience emotions outside pure despair, training your mind to access these states more readily.

However, it is normal that Substantial mental fortitude is required to not become disheartened or frustrated when your attempts to shift your emotional state fail to immediately provide relief. The key is to not give up. View it as brain training - you are actively trying to override years of neural patterning. With dedicated practice in not just shifting thoughts but finding positive emotion, the changes will come. Remind yourself regularly that if you stop making the effort to generate optimism, hope, and positivity, then the downward spiral of despair will undoubtedly prevail. Your chances are best if you keep working to change your emotional state, even if progress feels imperceptible.

Recognize that due to the negativity bias of the brain, it is far easier to shift into despair than the reverse. So be kind to yourself if hopefulness does not arise quickly. Do not become embittered that willing yourself to feel more positive emotions is challenging. Accept that this is a skill requiring time and commitment to master, but that it is eminently possible.

And remember that finding external support can reinforce the journey to hope. Whether counseling, support groups, religion, or friends, seek compassionate people who can nurture the seedlings of optimism arising within you. Their encouragement and perspective can help prevent you from losing faith when your own emotional state remains bleak. With tenacity and compassion, you can find light even in the darkest of times. But give yourself the grace to take it one step at a time - focus on shifting thoughts currently without demanding feelings transform instantly. If you persist, emotional change will follow.

The Five Biggest Obstacles That Will Prevent Us From Becoming the Positive You

1. Fear. As we discussed, anxiety, doubt, and worry can overwhelm optimism and hold you back from seeing the good. Managing fear is key.

2. Negative bias. Our brains tend to focus more on the bad over the good. Being aware of this tendency and consciously redirecting your thoughts can counteract it.

3. Old habits. Negative thinking can become automatic over time. Making a shift requires recognizing and interrupting those unhelpful patterns.

4. Lack of self-confidence. Believing you're incapable of change can become a self-fulfilling prophecy. Building self-efficacy helps.

5. Stress and fatigue. When demands outweigh resources, positivity is harder to maintain. Ensuring proper rest and work-life balance conserves mental energy.

6. Additionally, dwelling on the past, surrounded by critical people, or feeling a lack of control in life can also impede positive thinking. The good news is these obstacles are surmountable with self-awareness, focused effort to shift mindsets, and adopting habits that support a brighter outlook. It's a process, but very worthwhile.

Lifestyle Factors

Exercise is Not Just Good for the Body, It's Great for the Mind

Something that I, personally, enjoy, working-out. In my younger days, I played semiprofessional baseball, semiprofessional 'A' league softball, and I was a competitive powerlifter for years. Once the workout bug got into my system, it never left. Even today, I run a workout blog and have written a few books on specialized Isometric Programs. It's no secret that the body and mind work best when they work together. In closing, I wanted to point out how important exercise and working out has been to me for both my physical and mental recoveries. Let's break it down.

Exercise has been shown to have powerful effects on improving mood and alleviating symptoms of depression and anxiety. When we engage in physical activity, our bodies release endorphins, dopamine, serotonin and other neurotransmitters that can provide a natural 'high' and boost our moods. Additionally, exercise serves as a healthy coping mechanism for stress and difficult emotions. By channeling energy into physical movement, we give our minds a break from rumination and worry. This essay will provide details on how different types of exercise can help improve mood and mental health.

Aerobic Exercise

Aerobic exercises that raise your heart rate and breathing are one of the most effective types of exercise for improving mood. Activities like running, cycling, swimming, dancing, and kickboxing have demonstrated positive impacts on mood. Aerobic exercise releases endorphins, which act as natural pain relievers and can induce euphoria. It also stimulates neurotransmitters like serotonin, norepinephrine, and dopamine which are targeted by antidepressant medications. Studies strongly suggest that regular aerobic exercise can be as effective at treating mild to moderate depression as antidepressants and therapy. Just 30 minutes of aerobic activity 3-5 times a week has been shown to significantly reduce anxiety and depressive symptoms. The psychological benefits happen immediately after a workout and can last for several hours or days afterward.

Some mood-related benefits of aerobic exercise include:

- Releases endorphins, providing a natural high

- Reduces levels of the stress hormone cortisol

- Increases neurotransmitters targeted by antidepressants

- Enhances emotional regulation abilities

- Works as a healthy coping mechanism for stress

- Boosts self-esteem from achieving fitness goals

- Promotes better sleep which improves mood

- Provides distraction from worries and rumination

- Increases blood circulation and oxygen to the brain

For maximum mood benefits, studies suggest sustaining an elevated heart rate for at least 20-30 minutes numerous times per week. Mixing up the type of aerobic activity can help prevent boredom and training plateaus.

Strength Training

In addition to aerobic exercise, strength training with weights or resistance bands has also been shown to combat depressive symptoms effectively. Strength training releases endorphins similar to aerobics but also leads to physical changes like increased muscle mass and bone density, which can boost self-esteem. Building strength requires focus and helps distract from negative thoughts. It also improves self-efficacy and the ability to cope with life's stressors.

Research suggests strength training 2–3 times per week for 30–60 minutes can positively impact mood. Compound movements like squats, deadlifts, and presses that work major muscle groups cause the biggest endorphin surge. For optimal mental health benefits, make sure to give muscles days to recover between strength training sessions to prevent injury and burnout. Mixing up the exercises and the amount of weight/resistance used provides variation and helps maintain motivation.

Yoga

The mind-body practice of yoga combines physical activity with breathing exercises, meditation and deep relaxation. Studies show yoga can be extremely effective at improving mood, reducing stress and alleviating depression and anxiety symptoms.

Here are some mood-related benefits of a regular yoga practice:

- Releases endorphins and lowers the stress hormone cortisol

- Activates the parasympathetic nervous system to induce relaxation

- Improves emotional regulation and stress resilience

- Promotes mindfulness and distraction from rumination

- Decreases inflammatory immune responses that can worsen mood disorders

- Regulates hormones like gamma-aminobutyric acid (GABA) that are linked to mood

- Improves acceptance of oneself and life circumstances

- Enhances overall sense of well-being

For depression and anxiety, yoga practices that synchronize movement with breath are ideal. Flowing sequences like Vinyasa and Kundalini provide sustained aerobic benefits. Restorative and yin practices that hold gentle poses for several minutes cultivate relaxation. Practicing yoga consistently for many months provides the greatest improvements in mood. But even a single class can give an immediate mood boost.

Walking

One of the easiest yet effective forms of mood-boosting exercise is walking. Regular walking provides similar benefits as other aerobic activities like improving endorphin, serotonin, and dopamine activity. But it is low-impact and accessible to most people. Studies indicate that 30–60 minutes of brisk walking 3–5 times per week significantly reduces depressive and anxious symptoms. Cognitive processing during walking can also help improve mood by enhancing reflection and working through emotional challenges.

Some psychological benefits of incorporating more walking include:

- Improves endorphin and neurotransmitter levels

- Boosts self-esteem and feelings of self-efficacy

- Helps process emotions and thoughts

- Provides distraction from worries

- Reduces inflammation that can worsen depression

- Requires no equipment or gym membership

To reap the mood-enhancing results, sustaining an elevated heart rate with brisk continuous walking is key. Walking outdoors among nature or green spaces can amplify the mental health benefits. Listening to upbeat music or podcasts during the walk can also boost motivation and distraction from rumination.

High Intensity Interval Training (HIIT)

High intensity interval training (HIIT) involves short bursts of intense cardio exercise alternated with periods of rest and recovery. HIIT workouts provide similar mood benefits as other types of aerobic exercise. But the extremely vigorous high-intensity intervals further enhance endorphin and dopamine release, providing an extra mood boost. The varied routines and quick pacing of HIIT can also prevent boredom, which improves adherence.

Research on HIIT shows regular training can:

- Increase endorphin production, creating a runner's high

- Boost dopamine and serotonin levels

- Enhance overall sense of well-being

- Improve sleep quality which benefits mood

- Increase confidence and self-efficacy

- Provide distraction from negative thoughts

For optimal results, HIIT workouts should be 20–30 minutes long, including warmup and cool down. The high-intensity intervals should reach near maximum effort levels for 30–90 seconds, followed by 1-2 minutes of low intensity recovery. HIIT 2–3 times per week delivers the greatest mood improvements. It's important to include rest days between HIIT sessions to allow the body to recover and prevent overtraining.

Dancing

Dancing combines the mood-boosting effects of aerobic exercise with creative expression and social connection. The continuous movement to music provides sustained cardiovascular benefits, which releases feel-good endorphins. Learning and performing dance routines also redirects focus away from negative thoughts and worries. The social aspects of dancing can reduce isolation, which may worsen depression. Ballroom dancing with a partner can even enhance intimacy and bonding.

Research demonstrates that various dance styles including ballroom, Latin, hip hop, contemporary, ballet, and aerobic dance improve measures of happiness and reduce anxiety and depression. Consistently dancing 3–5 times per week for at least 30 minutes appears to provide the best mood benefits. Mixing up dance styles maintains enjoyment and motivation to continue a routine. Dancing with others can amplify the psychological benefits through social bonding and support.

Martial Arts & Combat Sports

Practicing martial arts and combat sports like boxing, kickboxing, karate, judo, wrestling, and mixed martial arts can also effectively boost mood and mental health. These activities provide vigorous aerobic benefits through technical drills, sparring, and competition that releases endorphins. The intense focus required while training cultivates mindfulness and distraction from rumination. Learning to apply controlled aggression also provides constructive emotional release. Combat sports build resilience and self-efficacy, which increases overall well-being. The social support and camaraderie with fellow athletes can also improve mood and reduce isolation.

Studies indicate regularly training and competing in martial arts and combat sports increases happiness while reducing depression and anxiety symptoms. The mental health benefits appear greatest when practicing 3–5 days per week for at least 30 minutes consistently over months and years. But even a single class can provide an immediate uplift through the endorphin surge. Competing provides motivation and feelings of accomplishment, which boosts self-esteem. Steady progression in training and achieving new skills and ranks enhances confidence and life satisfaction.

Outdoor Sports & Activities

Exercising and playing sports outdoors in green space and nature has been shown to provide even greater psychological benefits than indoor activity. Research suggests outdoor workouts improve mood, reduce anxiety and depressive symptoms, enhance motivation and vigor, and boost self-esteem. Exposing skin to sunlight triggers the release of serotonin, which improves mood. The varied sensory stimulation of being outdoors distracts from negative ruminating thoughts. Connecting with nature also reduces inflammation, blood pressure, and stress hormone levels. Group outdoor activities can reduce loneliness through camaraderie and social bonding.

Some examples of outdoor activities that boost mood include:

- Hiking - Releases endorphins and serotonin while surrounded by nature

- Tennis - Social sport improves motivation and reduces isolation

- Rock climbing - Fosters self-efficacy and mindfulness when focused on the present moment

- Golf - Provides mild aerobic benefits while immersed in nature

- Gardening - Rewards efforts with beauty while reducing stress hormones

- Stand-up paddleboarding - Fun balance sport surrounded by calming water

- Beach yoga - Holistic mind-body practice immersed in a soothing natural environment

In summary, research clearly demonstrates that regular exercise has potent antidepressant and anti-anxiety effects that can help improve mood and mental health. Aerobic activities, strength training, yoga, walking, HIIT, dancing, martial arts, combat sports, and outdoor recreation all provide physical and psychological benefits that alleviate depressive symptoms and enhance overall well-being. Aim for 20–60 minutes of exercise 3–5 days per week to reap the mood-related benefits. Mixing up the types of physical activity prevents boredom and increases enjoyment. Being active outdoors amplifies the positive impact on mental health. Using exercise as a healthy coping mechanism and making it a consistent habit is key for effectively combating negative moods and improving your sense of wellness.

Unconventional Forms of Exercise That Can Help Redirect Your Mood

Beyond traditional gym workouts, there are numerous unconventional physical activities that can also provide psychological and emotional benefits. Unique exercises that involve social interaction, creative expression, mindfulness, immersion in nature and recreation can positively impact mood, reduce anxiety and depression, enhance motivation and feelings of achievement, and promote overall mental wellbeing. This essay explores a wide variety of these unconventional mood-boosting exercises, along with examples of how to incorporate them into a routine.

Rollerblading

Gliding around on rollerblades provides an enjoyable mood-lifting aerobic workout outdoors. Balancing on the skates while propelling yourself forward engages the mind-body connection through intense focus and coordination. Learning new techniques like crossovers, turns and stops boosts feelings of success and self-confidence. Rollerblading with others facilitates social bonding. And cruising along scenic trails immerses you in calming natural scenery that enhances the mood benefits.

To reap the mental health benefits, aim for 45–60 minutes of recreational rollerblading 2–3 times per week. This could include blading on trails through parks or nature areas, around neighborhoods, or at outdoor rinks. Joining group skate meetups or lessons adds social motivation and support.

Hula Hooping

Twirling a hula-hoop around your body is a fun way to sneak exercise into your day that can also boost your mood. Coordinating the core muscles to keep the hoop spinning cultivates mind-body awareness. The playful, low-pressure nature makes it enjoyable regardless of skill level. Learning new moves and tricks provides a sense of achievement that increases confidence and self-esteem. The calming, meditative motion releases feel-good endorphins and reduces stress. And hooping to music adds an element of creative expression.

Aim to hula-hoop for 10–30 minutes daily. This can be done anywhere outdoors or indoors. Challenging yourself to learn new motions and techniques will maximize engagement, motivation, and mood benefits. Taking hoop dance fitness classes combines social interaction with skills progression.

Surfing

Catching and riding the waves while surfing provides both vigorous exercise and thrilling excitement that enhances mood. The full-body athleticism required improves strength, balance and endurance. The natural scenery creates a serene yet exhilarating setting. Mastering the proper techniques for paddling out, popping up and riding boosts feelings of success and confidence. Surfing with others fosters social bonding and camaraderie. And taking on bigger swells provides healthy adrenaline and satisfaction.

To reap the maximum mood boost, aim to surf 2-3 times per week for at least 60-90 minutes. This includes time paddling out to catch waves. Varied surf conditions and locations will keep it interesting. Taking lessons helps quickly gain skills. And joining a local surf club can motivate progression.

Slack-lining

Slack-lining involves carefully walking along a narrow, flat webbing strap tensioned a foot or two off the ground between two anchors. Balancing on the unstable line hones concentration, body awareness, coordination, patience, and mindfulness. Mastering new tricks builds confidence. Simply spending time outdoors in nature surrounded by trees can deliver mood benefits. And setting up a line at parks or beaches attracts curious people, sparking social connections.

Aim to practice slackline balancing 1-2 times per week for 30-60 minutes to relieve anxiety, reduce rumination, and boost positive emotions. This may involve mastering basic walking before progressing to turns, jumps, and poses. Joining group trick-line meetups can provide inspiration, support, and bonding.

Indoor Rock Climbing

The challenging puzzles involved in indoor rock climbing deliver both physical and mental boosts. Each climbing route requires strategic problem-solving to map handholds, footholds, and body positioning. The intense focus required hones concentration skills and cultivates mindfulness in the present moment. Reaching new heights and conquering harder climbs provides feelings of success and self-efficacy. Belaying partners fosters cooperation and companionship. And membership at a climbing gym provides access to exercise variety, social support and motivation.

For mood benefits, aim to climb challenging routes 2-3 times per week for at least an hour supplemented with yoga, weights or cardio. This could involve bouldering, top rope, lead or speed climbing. Changing up facilities prevents boredom and provides inspiration.

Handball

Handball is a fast-paced competitive wall-based ball sport that delivers vigorous mood-boosting exercise. The quick bursts of sprinting, pivoting, lunging and spinning increase strength, speed and endurance. Making diving saves and mastering wall passes hones coordination. Outmaneuvering opponents requires strategic thinking and mental toughness. Social bonding and camaraderie develop among teammates and competitors. And winning games delivers thrilling feelings of success and accomplishment.

To reap the mood benefits, play handball for 30–60 minutes 2-3 times per week at school gyms, recreation centers or against exterior walls. This can be singles, doubles or cutthroat with more players. Joining a recreational handball league adds regular social connection and competitiveness.

Hooping Classes

Group fitness classes centered around hula-hooping provide full-body aerobic exercise in a fun, carefree setting that improves mood. Students hoop to energetic music and learn skills like isolations, spins, escalators and body rolls facilitated by instructors. Creatively dancing with the hoops increases self-confidence. Progressing to longer and heavier hoops delivers feelings of achievement. The playful group atmosphere fosters bonding and reduces anxiety. And the meditative motion of hooping releases feel-good endorphins.

Take hooping classes 2-3 times per week for 45-60 minutes for maximal mood and fitness improvements. Having concrete skills to learn and master will maximize engagement and progress. Recruiting friends to join adds social motivation and support.

Bike Polo

Bike polo combines cycling with the team sport of polo for a fun, fast-paced game. Quick sprints and pivots on the bike improve cardiorespiratory fitness. Striking and maneuvering the ball with a mallet while navigating a bike requires intense coordination. Learning tricky ball handling skills like tail whips or handlebar dribbles builds confidence. Cooperation and communication with teammates fosters bonding. And informal tournaments provide friendly competition and feelings of achievement.

For a mood boost, play bike polo for 45-90 minutes 2-3 times per week. Joining a recreational team ensures regular games and new friendships. Improving ball handling and competitive strategies will maximize engagement and enjoyment.

Outrigger Canoeing

Paddling sleek outrigger canoes provides a vigorous arm workout surrounded by natural scenic views and immersion in Hawaiian culture. The coordinated team effort of synchronized stroking enhances bonding and synchronicity. Testing your endurance on longer distance paddling builds physical and mental fortitude. Learning to steer and balance the boat improves focus and concentration. Exposure to sun and saltwater provides mood-lifting sensory stimulation. And achieving new canoeing skills and goals boosts confidence and satisfaction.

For mood and fitness benefits, aim to paddle with a crew for 45-90 minutes 2-3 times per week. This may start on calm inland water before progressing to more challenging ocean courses. Joining a canoe club will ensure regular opportunities. And competitions add excitement and concrete accomplishments.

Circus Arts

Learning circus arts like aerial silks, trapeze, juggling, acrobatics and hand balancing requires intense focus, body control, discipline, and courage, which enhances mood and self-confidence. Mastering new skills and sequences boosts feelings of success and achievement. Creating graceful routines provides artistic expression. Being part of a circus troupe gives a sense of belonging and community. The novel thrills increase stimulation and aliveness. And regular training improves focus, coordination, strength, and endurance.

Take professional circus arts classes 2-3 times per week for 60-90 minutes, focusing on your favorite disciplines. Recruiting like-minded friends adds social support and inspiration. Performing for audiences delivers confidence-boosting excitement and fulfillment.

Slam ball

Slam ball combines basketball skills with goals placed 11 feet (3.35 m) above the ground, which requires jumping off trampolines to dunk. The explosive vertical leaps and hard landings build lower body strength and power. Sprinting and changing directions increases mobility. Nailing technical dunks provides feelings of mastery. Teamwork cultivates social bonding and support. And competing in intense games delivers mood-lifting adrenaline and accomplishment.

For mood and fitness benefits, playful court 5-on-5 slam ball for 45-60 minutes 2-3 times per week. Joining a recreational team ensures regular competitive play. And tourneys provide opportunities to test your skills against new talent.

Stand-Up Paddle boarding (SUP)

Paddling on a long, stable stand-up paddleboard provides full-body aerobic exercise surrounded by peaceful natural scenery. Maintaining balance on the board requires intense focus and concentration that redirects thoughts from worry. The soothing sound of water lapping improves serenity and relaxation. Mastering steering through ocean surf or rivers enhances self-efficacy. Paddling with groups fosters social bonding and support. And exploring new waterways maintains novelty and adventure.

For mood-enhancement, go Supping for 60–90 minutes 2–3 times per week on local lakes, rivers, or oceans. Taking lessons will quickly build skills. Joining a SUP meetup group encourages progression and camaraderie. Yoga paddleboarding adds flexibility training.

Axe Throwing

Tossing axes at distant targets provides mood-lifting feelings of success and accomplishment when you stick the bullseye. Achieving difficult trick shots improves self-confidence. The satisfying thud of a perfect throw delivers a visceral thrill. Social bonding develops while competing alongside others. And leagues provide an opportunity to test your ever-improving skills against new throwers. The intense concentration required for accuracy also cultivates mindfulness.

For optimal results, practice axe throwing at a range or your backyard for 45–60 minutes every week. Competing in a local recreational league will facilitate skills progression and excitement. Inviting friends for practice ensures motivating support.

Parkour

Parkour involves athletically navigating through outdoor urban environments by running, climbing, jumping and vaulting obstacles. Completing flowing sequences successfully boosts confidence and provides feelings of accomplishment. Concentrating on proper technique and precision fosters mindfulness. Training with a dedicated group enhances social bonding and support. Exposure to sunshine and nature while training improves mood. And mastering new skills and challenges builds mental fortitude and reduces anxiety.

To reap the benefits, practice parkour at outdoor courses for 60–90 minutes 2–3 times per week. Joining a group class or meetup will accelerate learning. Seeking new challenges prevents stagnation. And filming runs documents concrete progression.

Trampoline Fitness

High intensity interval workouts on trampolines provide a fun, low-impact form of exercise that improves mood through releasing endorphins, enhancing self-confidence and reducing stress. Jumping activates the lymphatic system, which detoxifies the body. Alternating explosive jumping with crunches and leg exercises delivers a full-body workout. Trying new skills like front flips or dunks provides thrilling accomplishment. The rebounding motion stimulates balance and coordination. And the bouncy surface is easy on joints while sculpting muscles.

For optimal results, bounce on a trampoline for 30–45 minutes 3–5 days per week following HIIT principles. Taking classes adds structure and social motivation. Setting new bouncing goals will maintain challenge.

Conclusion

In summary, unconventional physical activities that involve social connection, nature immersion, recreation, creative expression, mindfulness and learning new skills can provide unique psychological benefits beyond traditional gym exercise. Rollerblading, hula-hooping, surfing, slack lining, indoor climbing, handball, hoop classes, bike polo, outrigger canoeing, circus arts, slam-ball, standup paddleboarding, axe throwing, parkour and trampoline training are examples that can effectively improve mood. They can also reduce anxiety and depression, and enhance overall mental wellbeing and life satisfaction when incorporated into a routine.

The idea of using food to influence mood and spur happy thoughts certainly feels therapeutic, as your childhood memories can attest. Anecdotally, people have long claimed that favorite foods provide comfort and lift one's spirits. But what does the science actually tell us about using food to boost positivity and mental wellbeing?

Extensive research recently provides compelling evidence that your diet significantly impacts mood, outlook, and cognition. Both the short-term effects of individual meals and the long-term consequences of overall diet quality can shape your mental state. Scientists have uncovered the ways certain foods influence key neurotransmitters and neural pathways to combat stress, anxiety, and depression while boosting motivation, satisfaction, and positivity.

Serotonin, for example, is a critical neurotransmitter for mood regulation and feelings of calmness and happiness. Foods high in tryptophan, such as poultry, eggs, soybeans, nuts, seeds, and leafy greens, help the brain synthesize more serotonin. This is because tryptophan is converted to 5-HTP, which then forms serotonin. Even eating tryptophan-rich foods for a single meal can give serotonin levels a notable boost.

Similarly, the amino acid tyrosine, found in meat, dairy, beans, and nuts, is needed to produce dopamine and norepinephrine. These neurotransmitters are vital for focus, alertness, and drive. Tyrosine depletion leads to mental fatigue, while increased intake is linked to cognitive enhancement and ability to handle stress. Eating tyrosine-rich foods can quickly improve motivation and concentration.

Beyond specific amino acids, consuming foods high in prebiotics and probiotics has also demonstrated powerful effects on positivity via the gut-brain axis. Prebiotics, found in onions, garlic, bananas, greens, and whole grains, feed the healthy gut bacteria that produce mood-regulating neurotransmitters. Multiple studies reveal prebiotic intake reduces stress, anxiety, and negative thoughts while enhancing cheerfulness.

Probiotic foods like yogurt, kefir, kimchi, and kombucha contain beneficial organisms that positively influence communication along the gut-brain axis. Brain imaging shows consuming probiotics generates neurotransmitter activity in areas controlling emotion. Reviews conclude probiotics reliably decrease depression, rumination, social anxiety, and memory problems while improving outlook.

Research on polyphenol nutrients in cocoa, berries, coffee, and green tea uncovers yet another pathway food takes to brighten your mood. Polyphenols exert anti-inflammatory effects in the brain and prompt release of "feel good" neurotransmitters serotonin, dopamine, and endorphins. This reduces mental fatigue and nurtures a sunnier disposition. Regular cocoa consumption is especially effective for boosting positivity.

Beyond influencing neurotransmitter activity directly, foods also impact mental state via their effects on mental energy, blood sugar regulation, inflammation, and the stress response system. Refined carbs and sugary foods lead to crashes that promote irritability, anxiety, and depression. In contrast, foods with fiber, protein, and healthy fats provide sustained energy. Fish, avocados, olive oil, nuts, and dark chocolate are just a few options containing brain-boosting omega-3s and antioxidants for mental clarity and resilience against stress.

With this broad overview of the mechanisms involved, what are some specific examples of foods shown through research to lift mood and inspire happy thoughts?

Chocolate: Numerous studies confirm eating chocolate (especially dark chocolate with at least 70% cocoa) quickly improves mood, feelings of contentment, calmness, and overall wellbeing. Chocolate boosts neurotransmitters, reduces cortisol, and counters inflammation. Eating chocolate also directly stimulates the reward and pleasure centers in the brain.

Berries: Berries are packed with antioxidants that reduce inflammation in the brain and increase feel-good neurotransmitters. Blueberries, strawberries, and blackberries have all been shown to boost positivity, social connection, motivation, and cognitive function. Their polyphenols increase neural plasticity as well.

Walnuts: Rich in mood-enhancing tryptophan, antioxidants, and anti-inflammatory nutrients, walnuts are perhaps the top nut for elevating spirits. Just a handful has been shown to improve optimism, curiosity, motivation, and feelings of meaningfulness.

Green tea: The potent polyphenols called catechins in green tea increase dopamine and serotonin in the brain. Studies confirm just one cup rapidly improves mood while decreasing anger and depression. Drinking matcha green tea generates even stronger cognitive and mood benefits.

Fatty fish: Salmon, mackerel, sardines, trout, and other fatty fish are loaded with omega-3s that nourish neurotransmitter activity and combat inflammation underlying mood issues. Eating salmon several times a week is linked to nearly 30% lower rates of depression compared to those who rarely eat fish.

Bananas: Bananas contain tryptophan, but also work via being a prebiotic source of fiber that feeds probiotics. Unripe bananas in particular boost serotonin and reduce anxiety and sadness, according to research. Eating bananas helps shift outlook from pessimistic to optimistic.

Kimchi: This fermented cabbage condiment is packed with probiotics, shown to reduce social anxiety by an average of 25% in randomized trials. Kimchi also promotes cognitive resilience and reduces rumination compared to the placebo. The effects kick in within weeks of eating kimchi regularly.

Coffee: The caffeine and polyphenols in coffee increase levels of serotonin, dopamine, and noradrenaline according to research. This provides a mood and energy lift that can help you view circumstances more positively. Coffee improves outlook, self-esteem, motivation, and concentration.

The spinning instructor's positive words and energetic encouragement helped elevate her students' moods and build a sense of community, even during the most grueling parts of the workout. Her belief in each person helped them push through challenges and feel a sense of optimism. After class, people often walked out smiling and filled with happy endorphins.

The yoga teacher created an atmosphere of serenity and non-judgement. As students moved through poses, her soothing guidance helped quiet racing minds and build emotional balance. The emphasis on mindfulness, breath, and being present shifted focus away from negativity. Students left class feeling grounded and uplifted, carrying a greater sense of peace throughout their day.

The life coach listened deeply and reflected the client's strengths that she had lost sight of in her struggles. She highlighted past examples of resilience and integrity, reassuring the client that she had the inner wisdom to navigate this. Her supportive presence enabled the client to envision a way forward amid the uncertainty, awakening optimism and hope once more.

The bereavement counselor validated the deep pain of grief while providing the space to honor the complexity of emotions. Through empathetic listening and gentle guidance, she encouraged remembrance of the loved one without becoming mired in detachment or despair. Weeks later, clients expressed feeling the stirrings of positivity and meaning again.

The therapist provided a non-judgmental presence where clients felt safe to share freely without fear of rejection. She tuned into each person's authentic struggles, reflecting their emotions and uncovering hidden inner resources. Her unconditional positive regard built confidence and awakened self-compassion within the clients over time.

The mentor saw the potential within the struggling young man, even when he lost sight of it. She shared stories of her winding journey, reassuring him that setbacks and doubt are normal before finding purpose. Her warm encouragement empowered him to believe in himself again and take the next step.

The support group facilitated connection, realizing members were not alone in their daily challenges. The leader normalized struggles and reframed them as opportunities for growth when faced together. Laughter, empathy, and problem-solving emerged, reminding members of their inherent strengths and capacity for hope.

The conference speaker brought infectious optimism rooted in hard-won wisdom. He recounted early failures and disappointments on the path to success, emphasizing perseverance and passion. The audience left inspired to turn adversity into advantage and embrace a vision bigger than current circumstances.

The wise grandmother exuded unconditional love and reassuring certainty that all would be well. During the hardest times, her compassion shone through, reminding her grandchildren of brighter days ahead. Her presence was a calming refuge, building resilience to navigate each new challenge with optimism.

The joyful friend brought lightness that lifted spirits mired in negativity. His humor and enthusiasm shifted perspectives just enough for glimmers of hope to emerge. During moments of doubt or gloom, he reminded others that positivity and meaning are always within reach.

The veterans support community offered kinship built on shared experience of trauma and loss. But what emerged was greater than pain. Through camaraderie, vulnerability, and service, members felt the stirrings of purpose and possibility again. Their new mission was supporting each other's healing.

The young idealist arrived brimming with visionary solutions and steadfast belief in a better future. Her authentic passion ignited motivation in jaded teams, reminding them of their higher purpose. Soon, optimism emerged, even in the face of engrained obstacles. Progress felt attainable.

The spiritual leader guided connection to something bigger that realigned priorities and soothed anxiety. Through teachings, meditation, and counsel, he encouraged members to let go of past hurt and future worry. They described feeling waves of grace, hope, and inner peace not felt for years.

The dedicated teacher saw the potential within each student, even the disruptive ones. Through her firm compassion and words of affirmation, she coaxed it out. Students described how her unwavering belief lifted their ambitions and self-confidence over the school year.

The neighbor brought unexpected cheer through friendly chats and small acts of thoughtfulness. His quiet generosity of spirit during difficult times on the block was uplifting. Soon, neighbors united, reminding each other of shared humanity and resilience. Laughter overtook fear.

The community volunteer helped transform bleak and neglected city blocks by rallying residents to action. She motivated neighbors to come together for a common cause, reminding them pride and progress starts from within. Her enthusiastic vision ignited local optimism and revitalization.

There are Healthy and Happy Foods That Help Our Mind

Here is a list of 25 healthy foods that can also boost mental wellbeing and positive thoughts:

1. Salmon - High in omega-3 fatty acids that reduce inflammation and support brain cell growth. The healthy fats also boost neurotransmitters like serotonin that stabilize mood.

2. Blueberries - Contain anthocyanins that protect brain cells from oxidative stress. Blueberries improve signaling between brain cells to support cognition.

3. Broccoli - A source of mood-stabilizing magnesium. Broccoli is also rich in anti-inflammatory nutrients that improve communication between brain cells.

4. Walnuts - Loaded with mood-enhancing tryptophan, plant-based omega-3s, and antioxidants that stimulate new brain cell connections.

5. Asparagus - Rich in folate that helps regulate mood-influencing neurotransmitters like serotonin and dopamine. The prebiotics also feed good gut bacteria.

6. Dark Chocolate - Stimulates endorphin release and contains phenylethylamine, which acts as a mood lifter. Flavanols also improve blood flow and cognition.

7. Green Tea - Provides L-theanine, which increases levels of GABA, dopamine, and alpha waves in the brain associated with relaxation.

8. Turmeric - May boost serotonin and dopamine levels thanks to its active compound curcumin. Also exhibit potent anti-inflammatory effects.

9. Lentils - A source of slow-burning carbohydrates, protein and amino acids like tryptophan that support consistent energy and uplifted mood.

10. Kefir - A probiotic-rich drink that replenishes good gut bacteria tied to lower anxiety, depression, and stress-reactivity due to the gut-brain connection.

11. Spinach - Provides magnesium essential for neurotransmitter balance and vitamin C to support the production of stress-busting hormones.

12. Shiitake Mushrooms - Contains selenium, riboflavin, and antioxidants that improve anxiety and brain cell communication.

13. Grass-fed Beef - Amino acids like tyrosine help produce mood-boosting neurotransmitters dopamine and serotonin. Also, a bioavailable iron source.

14. Avocado - Stress-busting potassium and magnesium. Healthy fats improve absorption of mood-enhancing phytonutrients from other plant foods.

15. Kimchi - This fermented food contains probiotics that research shows reduce social anxiety, rumination, and aggression. Also boosts cognitive resilience.

16. Coffee - In moderation, provides caffeine that activates neurotransmitters for improved concentration, mood, and motivation. Antioxidants are also beneficial.

17. Wild-Caught Salmon - High in omega-3s EPA and DHA that lower inflammation and keep neuron cell membranes flexible for better signaling.

18. Bone Broth - Contains amino acids like glycine that act as neurotransmitters, boosting calmness and alleviating anxious thoughts.

19. Bananas - Improve the ratio of beneficial gut flora thanks to prebiotic fructooligosaccharides (FOS). Better gut health is tied to a positive mood.

20. Sweet Potatoes - Provide plenty of absorbable magnesium critical for neuron function and neurotransmitter balance to avoid depressive symptoms.

21. Seeds like Chia and Flax-Rich sources of thiamine, magnesium, and plant-based omega-3s to support cognitive health and uplifted mood.

22. Pistachios - Packed with protein, B6, and antioxidants. Also contain tryptophan and thiamine to boost gamma wave activity associated with calmness.

23. Dark Leafy Greens - Rich in folate, iron, and magnesium which play roles in dopamine and serotonin activity modulating mood and outlook.

24. Yogurt - Contains probiotics that improve communication along the gut-brain axis and reduces activity in brain areas linked to sadness and worry.

25. Sweet Potatoes - Provide mood-stabilizing vitamin B6, magnesium, fiber, and carbohydrates for an optimal glycemic response to avoid blood sugar crashes.

Taking the Big Soak, Steam Rooms and Hot Tubs

Steam rooms and hot tubs have been used for centuries as a way to promote relaxation, improve health, and lift mood. Modern research has now begun to uncover the scientific reasons behind these benefits.

One of the main ways steam rooms and hot tubs improve mood is by reducing stress and promoting relaxation. Stress causes the body to release cortisol and adrenaline, hormones that trigger the fight-or-flight response. Chronic stress leads to elevated cortisol levels, which can impair cognitive function, sleep, your mood, and the immune system. Spending time in a steam room or hot tub has been shown to rapidly reduce cortisol levels in the body. One study found a single session in a hot tub lowered cortisol by 31% in healthy young men. The warm water helps relax muscles, while the humidity of the steam room or hot tub helps promote deep breathing. This stimulates the parasympathetic nervous system, signaling the body to enter a state of calmness.

In addition to lowering stress hormones, steam rooms and hot tubs have also been found to increase levels of serotonin and dopamine in the brain. These are neurotransmitters that play key roles in regulating mood. Serotonin influences happiness, relaxation, and emotional stability. Dopamine is tied to motivation, pleasure, and the reward system. Multiple studies have shown that soaking in a hot tub increases blood circulation throughout the body, including in the brain. This boosts oxygen flow to the brain and provides an influx of dopamine and serotonin. Even just 10–15 minutes in a hot tub can increase dopamine levels by more than 30%, with the elevated levels lasting for hours afterward.

The combination of reduced stress hormones and increased feel-good neurotransmitters from using steam rooms and hot tubs produces measurable improvements in mood. One study asked participants to sit in a hot tub for 30 minutes, then assessed their psychological state afterward. They reported significant reductions in tension, confusion, anger, and depression, along with increased vigor. The positive effects lasted upwards of 4 hours afterward. Using a steam room or hot tub regularly trains the body to more easily enter into a relaxed state and provides lasting mood benefits.

In addition to mood, regular use of steam rooms and hot tubs has also been shown to improve cognitive function. The heat from steam and hot water activates the hypothalamus, which controls body temperature and influences brain function. Mild heat stress from being in a steam room or hot tub increases blood flow to the brain and raises brain temperature by around 1-2 °F. Even this subtle increase in brain temperature has been tied to improvements in focus, mental clarity, and decision-making abilities.

One study had participants alternate between sitting in a hot tub and then resting in room temperature air. Following 10 cycles of this, they completed cognitive tests. The group that had been exposed to the mild heat stress from the hot tub showed significant improvements in processing speed and performance on reaction time tests compared to the control group. Researchers believe the moderate heat activates neural networks in the pre-frontal cortex involved in attention, problem-solving, and impulse control. Another study that specifically looked at steam room use also found notable improvements in mental acuity and focus after sessions.

Using a steam room or hot tub before cognitively demanding tasks like work meetings, examinations, or mental exercises can boost blood flow to the brain and raise brain temperature, priming the central nervous system for optimal performance. The effects can last up to 2 hours afterward. With regular use over time, people report persistent improvements in their ability to think clearly and be mentally present.

The physiological changes produced by steam room and hot tub use also promote muscle relaxation and pain relief that can aid mental clarity. The warm environment facilitates muscle tissue release of built-up lactate that causes soreness and pain. Increased circulation carries away metabolic waste products that contribute to discomfort. And the buoyancy of water reduces strain on joints and pressure points. This reduction in muscle tension and pain can clear mental fog or distraction, allowing people to think and focus more intently.

Steam rooms and hot tubs also help fight inflammation in the body and brain that can impair cognition. Hyperthermic conditioning from exposure to heat stresses cells and tissues safely, triggering the release of heat shock proteins and anti-inflammatory cytokines. This provides lasting protection against inflammation-induced reductions in memory, focus, and mental endurance. Regular use of steam rooms and hot tubs trains the brain to more effectively regulate inflammatory pathways and their impact on neural function.

Overall, extensive research now confirms that incorporating steam room and hot tub sessions into a wellness routine can boost mood, reduce stress, enhance mental clarity, and prime the brain for optimal cognitive performance. The synergistic benefits come from improved circulation, muscle relaxation, anti-inflammatory effects, and specific neurotransmitter responses induced by warm water immersion and moist heat exposure. With routine use, steam rooms and hot tubs offer an accessible and effective way to support both emotional and mental wellbeing in the modern world.

I Have No Greater Love Than the One I Have For Our Animal Friends

Ode to the Animals Who Light Up Our Lives. I would like to share this with you. I searched for the author, but was unable to find their name.

My beloved friends with paws, hooves, fins, feathers, scales, and shells - how I cherish each of you. My life brims with joy because you are in it. You make this world a brighter, warmer place simply by being your perfect, wonderful selves.

I am endlessly grateful for all you do for my spirit. Your playful exuberance never fails to make me smile. Your tranquil presence settles my worries and fears. Your affection reminds me I'm worthy of love. You see me at my worst yet accept me with no judgment. You celebrate me at my best with no agenda beyond sharing in my happiness.

Not only that, but you ask so little yet give so much. A scratch behind the ears, a handful of feed, a cozy place to nest - simple comforts that mean the world coming from me. In return, you give me loyalty, laughter, purpose. You make me feel needed, trusted, respected. My day is complete only after soothing your sweet soul, too.

I promise to honor our bond by caring for you with gentle empathy. I will learn your unique language and needs. No matter what comes, we will face it together, side by side. You are family, woven permanently into the tapestry of my life.

Without you, my world would lose its color and music. My heart would beat to a duller rhythm. But with you, I see beauty everywhere and hear melodies that stir my spirit. My blood pulses with a zest for living that only your presence can ignite.

However, if we are gifted together, it will never be enough. Yet, I am endlessly grateful for the magical moments we share. Your light shines so brightly within me that, even when we are apart, I carry you along wherever I go. My life is blessed beyond measure for having crossed paths with you, if only for the brief while that is life.

Pets were used for therapeutic purposes in ancient history:

The Ancient Roots of Animal-Assisted Therapy

The use of animal companionship for therapeutic benefits stretches back thousands of years. Ancient cultures recognized the power of human-animal bonds to heal the mind, body, and spirit. Read on to learn how our ancestors used various creatures great and small as early forms of animal therapy.

Dogs as Healers in Ancient Egypt

Dogs held exalted roles in Ancient Egypt as protectors, hunters, herders, and healers. Egyptians observed how human contact with dogs lowered stress and anxiety. They brought dogs into temple rituals to create calm and comfort for supplicants seeking cures. Egyptians also placed dog figurines in tombs to protect souls in the afterlife. They recognized the spiritual significance of dogs' loyalty and intuitive abilities. Healing temples kept dogs as loving companions to lift people's moods and promote overall wellbeing.

Greeks Prescribed Riding for Health

The ancient Greeks were among the first to document the therapeutic value of horseback riding. Greek physician Hippocrates, known as the father of medicine, prescribed riding to improve circulation, muscle strength, and emotional health. The ancient Greeks noted how interacting with horses stimulated positive neurological and physiological responses that aided healing. Patients rode horses for mobility therapy, rehabilitation, and mood enhancement. The Greeks valued equestrian sports for promoting fitness, focus, self-esteem, and community participation.

Medieval Europeans Turned to Rabbits and Fish

During the Middle Ages in Europe, people began using small animals like rabbits, birds, lambs, and fish for therapy. Caring for these lovable creatures gave sick, lonely, and distressed individuals a sense of purpose. Stroking their soft fur and feathers helped calm anxieties. Watching their active, playful nature lifted spirits. Keeping small pets provided social support and distraction from pain. Monasteries and hospitals also stocked ornamental fishponds, finding the movement of bright fish soothing to observe.

Ancient Chinese Medicine Harnessed Animal Power

Traditional Chinese medicine recognized animals' healing energies. Tiger balm contained tiger bone for strength. Seahorse elixirs treated kidney disease. Rhino horns were believed to reduce fever. Chinese medicine also incorporated animals in mindfulness exercises. Practitioners prescribed visualized journeys with spirit animals for guidance. Patients undertook meditative fox walks through nature for mental acuity. Energy healing incorporates animal imagery and animal-derived medicines to restore harmonious flow. Chinese medicine used animal elements to enrich patients' mental and physical health.

Native Americans Found Spiritual Guidance in Animals

For Native Americans, animals carried deep spiritual meaning and offered wisdom. Tribes like the Ojibwe envisioned subconscious journeys into animal dreams or spirits to find focus, meaning, and healing. Totem poles featured animals like bears, wolves, and eagles to invoke their symbolic power. Native Americans captured the attributes of clever coyotes, tranquil deer, and stalwart buffalo to lead troubled minds toward insight and wholeness. Seeking animal guidance through shamanic rituals provided therapeutic release. Native Americans also kept dogs and horses as loyal companions to bolster emotional strength and resilience.

Ancient Civilizations Found Solace in Songbirds

The rich songs of birds inspired ancient peoples around the world. Chinese and Persian poetry extolled the beauty of songbirds. Egyptians used images of songbirds in hieroglyphics to represent the soul. Aristotle kept birds for pleasure; their melodies lifted his spirits. The ancient Roman thinker Marcus Aurelius found their music rejuvenating. Songbirds provided melodious therapy long before research proved birdsong's benefits. Our ancestors intuitively knew how nature's music could restore inner harmony and cheer.

The Hindus' Sacred Bond with Cows

Hindus traditionally supported an intimate bond with cows considered sacred. Caring for cows taught responsibility and mindfulness. The cows' calm, loving nature offered comfort and joy. Milk nourished the body, while their presence nourished the soul. Rubbing a cow's holy flanks relieved stress and anxiety. To this day, India's cow therapy centers provide respite from modern life's pressures through time with these gentle healers. The ancient Hindus revered cows as divine maternal figures representing life's soothing rhythms.

Pets Through the Ages

From ancient Egyptians to Native Americans, early societies shared meaningful bonds with animal companions. Dogs, horses, cows, birds, fish, rabbits, and other creatures transmitted their grounding and uplifting energies. Our ancestors intuitively grasped animals' abilities to calm minds, inspire spirits, and restore health. Today's widespread use of prescribed emotional support animals and clinical animal therapy extends an ancient recognition of nature's healing gifts. Our longtime interspecies connections remind us we are all fellow passengers sharing life's journey.

The Positive Power of Pets: How Our Furry Friends Improve Our Mental Health

Pets have been by our sides for thousands of years. From dogs assisting us with hunting and guarding to cats catching mice in our homes, these domesticated animals have provided many practical benefits. But perhaps their greatest gift is to our mental health and overall wellbeing. Science has shown that pets can reduce stress, anxiety, and depression while increasing joy, social connection, and even our longevity. Read on to learn how our furry, feathered, and finned friends make our lives better in so many ways.

The Calming Power of a Purr

It's no secret that petting or playing with a cat can melt away stress. But research has uncovered that a cat's purr delivers calming effects on the body and mind. Studies found that frequencies in purring fall in the 20-140Hz range and can have therapeutic effects like promoting bone growth, wound healing, and pain relief. The rhythmic vibrations of a purr may physically alter our nervous system, reducing blood pressure, heart rate, and anxiety. Kitties often purr during positive social interactions with humans or when nursing their young. So next time your cat curls up on your lap and starts to purr, let the relaxing rhythm soothe your worries away.

The Joy of Puppy Love

Few things bring more pure joy and comfort than a happy puppy. Their playful energy and unconditional love can brighten the gloomiest mood. One study measured participants' hormonal responses after interacting with dogs. They found increased levels of oxytocin, prolactin, phenylacetic acid, and dopamine - hormones and neurotransmitters associated with bonding, trust, pleasure, and wellbeing. Even short interactions with dogs provide mood-lifting benefits. Therapy dogs are also used to comfort those grieving or experiencing trauma and help children with emotional disorders open up. If you need a pick-me-up, try spending time with a bubbly pup. Their magnetic positivity is sure to rub off on you.

Feathered Friends Fight Depression

Having a bird as a pet may help ward off depression and anxiety, according to research. A study followed over 400 adults and found that bird owners had better mental health, including lower rates of depression, stress, and tension. Caring for a bird gives a sense of purpose and teaches responsibility. Watching their beauty and silly antics also boosts moods. Listening to birdsong and music lowered depression scores in another study. So, tuning into your parakeet's melodies could positively impact your state of mind. Consider adopting a tweeting companion if you're feeling blue.

The Motivating Love of a Dog

Dogs have a special talent for motivating and energizing their humans. A study had children read aloud in front of peers, teachers, and a dog. The students displayed far less stress when reading to the nonjudgmental canine audience. Their presence motivates us to get outside, socialize, and live more actively. Having a consistent routine of walking, playing, training, and caring for a dog gives meaning and purpose. Their unconditional affection also makes you feel appreciated and lifts self-esteem. Seniors with dogs have better physical and mental health and visit doctors less frequently. No matter your age, a dog's friendship inspires you to live your best life.

Scaly Stress Relief

Reptile lovers can attest that scaly critters make surprisingly soothing pets. Despite their cold-blooded reputation, snakes, lizards, tortoises and turtles offer comfort and stress relief. Their calm nature and enjoyable routines of feeding and handling create relaxation. Watching their graceful movements is mesmerizing, much like meditating with flowing candles or water fountains. The novelty factor of exotic reptiles also takes your mind off worries by transporting you to a tropical paradise whenever you observe or hold them. If you find the presence of more conventional pets like cats and dogs overstimulating, a reptilian roommate could be the perfect Zen companion.

The Social Bonding Power of Pets

Human-animal relationships can satisfy our fundamental need for social connection. For those living alone, pets provide much-needed companionship. Studies show that older adults with pets feel less lonely and have an easier time connecting with others. Sharing the love for your cat or talking about your dog's silly antics builds relationships. Walking your pup also leads to outdoor social encounters you may miss otherwise. At nursing homes, fish tanks promoted more socialization and improved eating habits of Alzheimer's patients. Pets act as social facilitators and conversation starters, bringing more engagement and joy to our lives.

Furry Friends for Focus and Flow

Have you ever noticed how caring for pets brings a sense of mindful presence? When you're engaged in petting, feeding, training, or playing with animal companions, you're pulled into a flow state of focus and joy. Stressful thoughts fade away as you become absorbed in living in the moment with your furry therapist. Therapeutic horseback riding helps disabled patients improve posture, balance, and self-confidence. Equine therapy also benefits people with PTSD, anxiety, depression, and autism. Caring for any pet increases oxytocin and dopamine levels in the brain, bringing calm and happiness. They ground us in mindful continuity from moment to precious moment.

The Healing Power of Fishy Zen

Watching brightly colored fish glide elegantly through water is profoundly relaxing and meditative. Aquariums are even used in medical settings like dental offices to calm nervous patients. Research shows that viewing aquarium displays lowers blood pressure, reduces anxiety, and improves mood. The hypnotic aquatic movements and tranquil soundscapes create a Zen-like ambiance. The presence of fish tanks helped ease anxiety in Alzheimer's patients during mealtimes, reducing the need for nutritional supplements. Aquatic life offers healing serenity. Consider adding a fish tank to your home for a daily dose of underwater Zen.

Pets Promote Longevity

Not only do pets bring us joy day-to-day, they actually help us live longer lives. Studies show that owning pets, especially dogs, comes with a lower risk of cardiovascular disease. Dog parents have lower cholesterol, triglycerides, and blood sugar levels. Stroking soft fur comforts the nervous system. One study found that heart attack patients who owned pets had better survival rates a year later compared to non-pet owners. People with pets visit the doctor less and have lower rates of depression. Companion animals encourage healthy behaviors and give affection we need to thrive. The social support, movement, and unconditional love they provide protects our hearts and adds years to our lifespan.

The Takeaway

Abundant research confirms what pet lovers already know - our animal companions greatly enrich our lives. From relieving loneliness to motivating us to reducing anxiety and depression, pets boost our mood, health, and vitality in so many ways. Caring for animals also develops empathy, responsibility, and routine. The joyful presence of pets helps us be more mindful, present, and socially connected. If you're considering getting a pet, adopt a four-legged friend, feathered fellow, or finned fishy into your family. Your heart and mind will thank you.

Conclusion

Closing Thoughts

Focusing on the positive rather than miring in the negative is ultimately uplifting and nourishing for the human spirit. It also has tangible benefits for both mental and physical health. The simple yet powerful techniques covered in this book provide practical tools to train your mind to default to a more optimistic perspective.

When you make a consistent habit of gratitude journaling, repeating affirmations, visualization exercises and other positive thinking practices, you physically rewire your brain over time. The neural pathways associated with resilience, creativity and possibility are strengthened through frequent use. Automatic negative thought patterns fade as those connections atrophy from disuse. Though it takes some discipline initially, choosing positivity soon becomes your brain's reflexive go-to response.

Ruminating on problems, faults and worst-case scenarios puts the brain in a state of chronic stress. This reinforces unhelpful thought patterns stemming from a scarcity mindset of lack, helplessness and victimhood. Dwelling in negativity saps motivation, fuels anxiety and raises cortisol levels that strain the body. It becomes a self-fulfilling prophecy as you expect the worst and fail to take action.

Conversely, focusing on solutions, personal strengths and possible breakthroughs unlocks creativity, productivity and inner resources needed to overcome challenges. Having a positive mindset primes you to be alert to opportunities and bold in pursuing meaningful goals. Positivity provides the courage and grit to view obstacles as temporary setbacks to work through rather than insurmountable failures.

Studies show optimistic individuals have reduced risk of cardiovascular disease, lower blood pressure and less inflammation than their pessimistic counterparts. Positivity and joyful emotions boost the immune system and natural killer cell activity, while chronic stress from negative thinking suppresses immunity. People who score high in traits like gratitude, curiosity and emotional stability enjoy greater longevity.

Negativity and constant worrying generate harmful levels of cortisol and adrenaline that course through the body. This leads to fatigue, muscle tension, headaches and poor sleep over the long term. Critics are more prone to skin conditions like eczema and dermatitis as stress manifests physically. Negative rumination and anger also raise your risk of stroke and headaches.

Beyond physical repercussions, negativity colors how you interpret events and interactions. Pessimists develop cognitive distortions where they automatically discount positives and magnify negatives. This skewed perception reinforces the outlook that life is stacked against you. Positivity allows you to put things into a constructive perspective and see impediments as temporary setbacks.

Staying Positive is Not Easy, It Will Take Work and Practice to Stay Positive in a World of Craziness

The pressures and turbulence of modern life make it extraordinarily difficult to maintain a consistently positive mindset. We face a barrage of stressors including work demands, financial strain, information overload, health crises, social isolation, environmental degradation, and pervasive negativity across media channels. This daily torrent of adversity wears down even the most optimistic spirit. It can feel nearly impossible to stay positive when overwhelmed by looming responsibilities, inescapable problems, and unpredictable chaos.

However, while maintaining an upbeat attitude through all of life's trials requires tremendous mental strength and discipline, it is certainly possible. With intentional practices, sufficient social support, and perspective from past experience, you can build resilience against the toxic effects of negativity. But it takes vigilance. Our brains have evolved to fixate more readily on the negative as an adaptive survival mechanism. Overcoming this negativity bias demands conscious effort.

Practicing gratitude is foundational - appreciating what you have versus dwelling on perceived lacks. Expressing thanks, even for small joys like a warm cup of coffee, focuses your mind away from fear or frustration. Maintaining gratitude journals re-wires neural pathways to perceive positivity despite challenges.

Surrounding yourself with uplifting people provides a wellspring of encouragement when your own reserves run low. Their energy and outlook can help reignite optimism just when you need it most. Seek kindred spirits who uplift you rather than join in commiseration.

Establishing daily rituals builds resilience against the emotional ups and downs. Whether it's morning meditation, mid-day walks outdoors, or creative hobbies, carve out time to let stress melt away and renew perspective. Make self-care priorities like nutrition, sleep, and exercise the center of your days instead of allowing them to get crowded out.

Set clear boundaries around media consumption and news intake. Be judicious regarding when and how much you expose yourself to the endless flow of negativity across devices and channels. Use tools to filter and curate your information ecosystem in healthy ways. Unplug regularly for full digital detoxes.

Challenge catastrophic thinking when your mind makes exaggerated projections about worst case scenarios. Ask yourself, realistically, how likely is the terrible outcome you are envisioning? Reframe the situation into a growth opportunity. Remember most crises contain seeds of transformation.

Recall past examples of resilience and breakthrough during dark times. When current struggles seem endless, reflect on when you previously navigated hardship or found light in darkness. You've summoned positivity before - you can do it again now. Have faith in the ever-changing nature of circumstances.

Avoid downward social comparison and the illusion of perfection in other people's lives. Focus on your gifts rather than measuring yourself against others. Comparison breeds resentment and defeat. Walk your unique path and define success on your terms.

Finally, view positivity as a muscle that strengthens with training. The more you practice overriding negative biases, limiting beliefs, and pessimistic rumination, the more automatic those positive habits become. You can literally remodel neural connections through intention and repetition. But persistence is mandatory.

While maintaining buoyancy and cheer always remains challenging in our complex world, Lifetime wisdom confirms that hope, meaning; contentment do emerge for those brave enough to expect light even in the darkest of nights. But finding positivity requires vigilance. It won't arise by wishing. Through courage, flexibility, and daily practice, even the stormiest seasons can be endured and ultimately transformed. A positive mindset relies not on circumstances, but the determination to seek beauty and opportunity when all seems bleak. With commitment to this discipline, serenity and optimism can prevail even amid the swirling chaos. By investing just a few minutes a day practicing the positive thinking techniques presented in this book, you can gradually reorient your brain's habitual perspectives. Simple shifts like writing down grateful moments, reciting uplifting affirmations, imagining your ideal future self, and replacing negative phrases with positive ones will accumulate over time to recreate your psyche and life outlook.

With consistent practice, positivity becomes your default personal reality - how you operate, create, interact. While negative thoughts will still sporadically arise, they become passing clouds rather than long-term storms. You develop the mental flexibility to pivot your mindset back to the constructive when negativity strikes. With this resilience, you are freed up to live a rich, meaningful life aligned with your deepest truths. The choice is yours - scatter seeds of positivity or negativity daily, then witness as they blossom over time.

It is All in the Science, Don't Just Take My Word

Medical studies on the benefits of positive thinking dating back to the 1970s:

1. A 1977 study published in Psychosomatic Medicine looked at type A behaviors and cardiovascular health in over 100 male lawyers. They found that optimism and positive expectations were associated with reduced risk of heart issues over the 8.5-year follow-up. This early study was conducted by researchers at Stanford University.

2. A 1979 study in Psychosomatic Medicine followed 225 Harvard students for 35 years. They found students with more positive explanatory styles and optimism had better physical health later in life. This influential long-term study was done by researchers at the University of Pennsylvania.

3. A 1988 study in the Journal of Personality and Social Psychology looked at positive affect and susceptibility to the common cold in over 300 healthy volunteers. They found that increased positive emotional style was associated with greater resistance to developing colds. This study was conducted by researchers at Carnegie Mellon University.

4. A 1997 study in the Mayo Clinic Proceedings followed over 800 older adults for 5 years. They found that optimistic elderly individuals had better health outcomes including reduced risk of early death compared to pessimistic individuals. This study was done by researchers at Yale University.

5. A 2003 meta-analysis published in Psychological Bulletin reviewed 150 studies on benefit finding and growth after trauma. They concluded that people often report benefits like changed priorities, closer relationships, and spiritual development after traumatic events. This comprehensive analysis was led by researchers at the University of North Carolina.

6. A 2009 study in Applied Psychology followed over 1,000 healthy adults for 9 years. They found that positive expectations about aging helped protect against risks from accumulated life stresses. This longitudinal study was conducted by researchers at Yale University.

7. A 2011 study in Health Psychology looked at psychological resilience and found optimism was linked to faster cardiovascular stress recovery. This experiment was conducted by researchers at the University of Illinois.

8. A 2015 study published in the Journal of Behavioral Medicine looked at the effects of positive thinking on wound healing in 90 adults. Participants who scored higher on optimism scales had faster wound healing than those with lower optimism scores. This study was conducted by researchers at the University of Texas.

9. A 2016 study in the Journal of Aging and Health followed over 4,000 older adults for up to eight years. They found that individuals with more positive self-perceptions of aging lived longer than those with more negative self-perceptions of aging, even after controlling for actual health conditions. This large longitudinal study was conducted by researchers at Yale University.

10. A 2019 study published in JAMA Network Open followed over 69,000 women for 10 years. They found that women with higher optimism scores were significantly more likely

to achieve healthy aging, defined as being free of major chronic diseases and having good mental health and no major cognitive, physical, or mental limitations. This study was conducted by researchers at Harvard University.

In Closing a Thank You to My Friends

Life will inevitably thrust you into the crucible that tests your mettle. How you respond during those times means everything it decides if you crumble or rise and reforge stronger. I learned this truth through relentless storms that battered me over decades. Now I share with you about the inner power that fueled me through those darkest nights, so you too can ignite your inner light when tested.

For over 20 grueling years, I actively forged an armor to steel myself for the battles ahead. I voraciously studied techniques to fortify my mindset – positive thinking, visualization, meditation, NLP, perfecting mind-body health, and more. Initially these were just survival tactics to endure repeated traumas of surgeries, treatments, and harrowing diagnoses. But eventually, I realized these principles held magic to empower anyone to defy the odds.

We all have deep reservoirs of resilience within if we consciously master our mindset. By facing anguish with defiant hope instead of despair, we gain the might to conquer even the most menacing demons. Practicing gratitude, optimism and self-belief makes us more resilient when life throws us off course.

I authored this book to reveal how positive psychology ignited my own healing and growth through harrowing health crises. I had access to the great medical care when facing brain cancer, multiple orthopedic reconstructions, and other daunting diagnoses. But medicine alone could not account for my survival and continued ability to thrive. These positive mental techniques enabled me to overcome what medicine alone could not. If they empowered me through those times of despair, they could help anyone transcend whatever seeks to break them.

My call to share these lessons came from an unlikely voice – my lifelong friend Tim "Big Daddy." Just days after my second hip replacement Tim texted me: "Of all the guys I know, you're the toughest bastard hands down." His words crystallized that my journey could inspire others facing their own troubling times. Tragically, Tim passed weeks later from a sudden heart attack, leaving a hole in my heart. But his message will always live on, motivating me to pass these insights to you.

Reshaping your mindset takes grit, as it means battling the demons that have ruled you for years. You must pry loose despair's viselike grip and supplant it with empowering, uplifting truth. This mental rebirth is the hardest work I've ever undertaken, but also the most crucial. With ironclad resolve to shift your lens, you will unearth reserves of strength you never imagined.

The techniques I share will coach you through rebuilding your mind's circuitry. Visualize desired outcomes. Reframe setbacks as fuel for growth. Allow positivity to pierce even your bleakest moments. Meet anguish with purpose and troubles with hope. Leaning into the storm forges resilience. You can endure even the unendurable and come out on the other side.

So, when challenges back you into a corner, roar back "I Can, I Will, I Must, persist!" My arduous journey proves we can master adversity if we command our perspective. Dark forces must yield to the beacon within. Have courage, stand firm in self-belief, and let tenacious hope illuminate your path. You have the power to thrive through affliction and chart your odyssey. Uplift your mindset and make positivity your prophecy.

The road is long and demanding. But I promise you, light always overcomes darkness. From the deepest sorrow, we can rise renewed. When you feel defeated, draw strength from those who came before. Let the flicker inside you grow into an inferno. This is the purpose we are called to do, leave the trail a little brighter for those who follow when we are gone.

My own fire was lit from an early age. My mother instilled in me the faith that I could achieve whatever I envisioned through passion and hard work. My father constantly tore me down by always saying that I would amount to nothing, I had no skill to be successful. I lived with those two conflicting messages growing up. I channeled that drive into sports, earning a sports award that opened doors. As an avid reader of psychology books on NLP, Visualization, Meditation, Positive Thought, Exercise and Eating, properly I saw healing transcend medicine alone. These insights compelled me to share the mindset lessons that served me through my darkest hours.

I'm not a doctor, nor do I claim to be. I don't pretend my techniques are the only way. But they empowered me to thrive through dozens of surgeries, harrowing diagnoses, and loss. My friend saw something in my journey that spoke to the resilience of the human spirit. I hope by sharing it, I can light the way for you too, whenever the night seems darkest. Stay strong. Have faith. Your light remains as bright as ever. Keep walking towards it one step at a time. You can do this, there is no question in my mind!

Kevin

Glossary of Positive Words

Acceptance - The act of receiving something offered, with approval or favor.

Actualization - The realization or fulfillment of one's talents and potentialities.

Affirmation - A declaration that states something positively to be true.

Altruism - Unselfish concern for the welfare of others.

Ameliorate - To make or become better, more bearable, or more satisfactory.

Amnesty - A pardon extended by the government to a group or class of people.

Anticipation - The act of looking forward or anticipating the future.

Appreciate - Recognize the full worth of something.

Aspiration - A hope, ambition, or goal.

Assurance - A positive declaration intended to give confidence.

Aura - The distinctive atmosphere or quality that seems to surround a person or thing.

Autogenous - Originating within the body or from internal causes.

Beneficence - The doing of good, actively improving the life of others.

Benevolence - An inclination to perform kind, charitable acts.

Bliss - A state of extreme happiness and contentment.

Catharsis - The process of releasing pent-up emotions to relieve tension.

Catalyst - A person or thing that precipitates an event or change.

Cathartic - Providing psychological release through the open expression of emotions.

Centering - The process of calming the mind and focusing within.

Charity - Generosity towards those in need, an act of selfless giving.

Clairvoyance - Supposed ability to see things beyond the range of normal perception.

Coherence - The quality of being logical, consistent, and intelligible.

Comfort - A state of physical ease and freedom from pain or constraint.

Commendation - An official act of approval or praise.

Commitment - A pledge or promise to do something.

Compassion - Sympathetic consciousness of the distress of another.

Concentration - The ability to direct one's thinking or focus exclusively on one subject.

Conciliation - The easing of anger or hostility through calmness and self-control.

Confidence - A feeling of trust in someone or something.

Congruity - Agreement, harmony, conformity, or correspondence.

Conscience - The inner sense of what is morally right or wrong.

Consciousness - The quality or state of awareness, having a subjective experience.

Contemplate - Look thoughtfully for a long time at something.

Contentment - A state of happiness and satisfaction.

Contrition - Sincere remorse or guilt over one's misdeeds or failures.

Convalescence - The gradual recovery of health and strength after illness.

Conviction - A firmly held belief, opinion, or principle.

Courage - The ability to confront fear, difficulty, intimidation, or pain.

Courtesy - Polite behavior and excellence of manners.

Creativity - The use of imagination or original ideas to create something.

Deliberation - Careful thought and consideration before making a decision.

Delight - Great pleasure, joy, or satisfaction.

Dignity - Calm, ethical, restrained behavior deserving of respect.

Discernment - The ability to make careful judgments and form astute opinions.

Discipline - Training that corrects, molds, or perfects mental faculties or moral character.

Discovery - Finding or learning something for the first time.

Dream - A series of thoughts, visions, or feelings that occur during sleep.

Elation - An exhilarating psychological state of joy and pride.

Empathy - The ability to understand and share another person's feelings.

Encouragement - The act of inspiring others with confidence, hope, and courage.

Endorphins - Hormones released by the brain to relieve pain or improve mood.

Energize - Give vigor and enthusiasm to someone or something.

Enlighten - Give greater knowledge, insight, or awareness to someone.

Enthusiasm - Great excitement and eagerness for something.

Epiphany - A sudden manifestation or realization of something.

Equanimity - Composure and calmness, especially under tension or stress.

Esteem - Favorable opinion or judgment about someone or something.

Eternity - Infinite or unending time.

Euphoria - An intense feeling of happiness, confidence, or well-being.

Exaltation - The action of raising someone in rank, character, or status.

Excitement - The feeling of lively enthusiasm and eagerness.

Exhilaration - A feeling of lively joy, excitement, or elation.

Existence - The state of continuing to be real; actual presence.

Exultation - Great joy or delight; elation.

Faith - Complete trust or confidence in something or someone.

Fidelity - Faithfulness or loyalty to a cause, oath, commitment, or obligation.

Forgiveness - The action of pardoning someone for a mistake or wrongdoing.

Fortitude - Strength of mind enabling one to meet danger with courage.

Freedom - The power to act without constraint; liberty of action.

Friendship - A relationship of mutual affection between two people.

Fulfillment - The achievement of something desired, promised, or predicted.

Generosity - Willingness to give money, time, resources, or help to others.

Gentleness - The quality of being kind, tender, or mild-mannered.

Grace - Elegant movement, poise or balance.

Gratification - Pleasure, satisfaction, or delight.

Gratitude - The quality of being thankful and appreciative.

Gusto - Great energy, enthusiasm, and enjoyment.

Harmony - Agreement or accord; congruity.

Healing - The process of making or becoming sound, healthy, or whole again.

Health - The state of being free from physical illness or injury.

Honesty - The quality of being truthful, trustworthy, and sincere.

Hope - A feeling of expectation, desire, and trust.

Humanitarian - Concerned with or seeking to promote human welfare.

Ideal - Existing as an archetypal idea, model, or aspiration.

Illumination - Spiritual or intellectual enlightenment.

Imagine - Form a mental image of something not present to the senses.

Immunity - Protection from a disease or harmful condition.

Improve - To make or become better in quality, condition or appearance.

Incentive - Something that motivates or encourages someone to do something.

Insight - Deep understanding, self-awareness, or wisdom.

Inspiration - A sudden brilliant or creative idea or impetus.

Intention - Something intended; an aim; a plan.

Intuition - The ability to understand something instinctively.

Joy - A feeling of pleasure, contentment, happiness and satisfaction.

Justice - The upholding of moral rightness; equity.

Kindness - The quality of being friendly, generous, and caring.

Knowledge - Information and skills acquired through learning and experience.

Laughter - The act of laughing, an expression of joy or amusement.

Liberation - The act of setting someone free from confinement or oppression.

Lucidity - Clear and easy to understand; intelligible.

Luck - Success that seems to happen by chance.

Maturity - Fully developed character or abilities.

Meditation - Focusing the mind to increase awareness, insight and relaxation.

Mercy - Compassion shown to an offender by not punishing them severely.

Metamorphosis - A complete transformation or marked change in appearance.

Mindfulness - Maintaining awareness of one's thoughts, emotions and experiences.

Miracle - An extraordinary event attributed to divine intervention.

Mirth - Amusement, merriment or laughter.

Modesty - The quality of being humble and moderate in opinion of oneself.

Motivation - Willingness to do something; enthusiasm.

Mysticism - Belief in or experience of a reality beyond normal perception.

Nirvana - In Buddhism, a transcendent state free from suffering and desire.

Nobility - Having fine personal qualities and high moral principles.

Nurture - To care for, feed, and protect someone or something tenderly.

Objective - Uninfluenced by emotions or personal prejudices.

Observation - Careful watching and listening, studying, or noting facts.

Openness - Ready to entertain new ideas; unprejudiced; receptive.

Optimism - Hopefulness and confidence about the future.

Paradise - A place of beauty, delight, or happiness.

Passion - Strong enthusiasm or desire for something.

Patience - The capacity to accept or tolerate problems or suffering.

Peace - A state of tranquility, quiet, calm, or harmony.

Perception - Insight or intuition gained through the senses.

Perfection - The highest degree of proficiency or excellence.

Perseverance - Steady persistence in adhering to a course of action.

Perspective - An attitude toward or way of regarding something.

Piety - Reverence for God and devout fulfillment of religious obligations.

Positivity - Having a positive attitude, emphasizing the good.

Potential - Capable of developing into something in the future.

Prayer - Communication with a deity, either aloud or silently.

Presence - The state of existing or being present in a place.

Prosperity - Success in financial or material matters; flourishing.

Prudence - Careful forethought to avoid harm or risk.

Purity - Freedom from anything that debases, contaminates, or pollutes.

Purpose - The reason for which something exists or is done.

Realization - Full understanding or comprehension of something.

Reconciliation - The restoration of friendship between people after discord.

Recover - Regain health and strength after illness or weakness.

Redemption - Being saved from sin, error, or evil.

Reflection - serious thought or consideration about something.

Reform - Make changes for improvement; amend by removal of faults.

Rejoice - Feel or show great joy or delight.

Relaxation - The act of making less tense, tight, rigid, or stiff.

Reliability - Consistently good in performance or quality.

Relief - A feeling of reassurance following a period of anxiety or distress.

Renewal - An instance of resuming an activity after a pause.

Repose - A state of rest, sleep, tranquility, or recreation.

Resilience - The capacity to recover from difficulties or toughness.

Resolution - Firm determination to do or not do something.

Respect - Due regard for the feelings or rights of others.

Responsibility - Obligation to deal with or take care of something.

Restoration - A return to an earlier good condition or position.

Reverence - A feeling of profound awe and admiration.

Revitalize - Give new energy or vitality to something or someone.

Revival - An improvement in condition or strength after a decline.

Sacrifice - Willingly forgo or give up something valued for a goal.

Salvation - Being saved or protected from harm, risk, or loss.

Sanctuary - A place of refuge, protection, or safety.

Satisfaction - Fulfillment of a need or desire; contentment.

Security - The state of being free from danger or threat.

Self-esteem - Confidence in one's own worth or abilities.

Self-respect - Due regard for one's own character and conduct.

Serenity - The state of being calm, peaceful, and untroubled.

Service - Work done for others as an act of goodwill or devotion.

Simplicity - The quality of being easy to understand or uncomplicated.

Sincerity - Free from pretense or deceit; proceeding genuinely and honestly.

Solace - Comfort received when feeling grief or misfortune.

Solidarity - Unity arising from shared interests or feelings.

Solitude - The state of being alone or remote from others.

Spirituality - Concern for that which transcends the physical.

Stability - Resistance to sudden change or deterioration.

Strength - The capacity to withstand great force or pressure.

Success - Favorable outcome of attempting to achieve an aim.

Support - To uphold, defend, back up, or reinforce someone or something.

Sympathy - Understanding between people; common feeling.

Temperance - Moderation or voluntary self-restraint in action or statement.

Thankfulness - Conscious of benefit received; appreciative.

Therapeutic - Having healing properties; curative.

Thought - An idea or opinion produced by thinking.

Tolerance - A fair and permissive attitude toward those different from oneself.

Tranquility - A state of peace, quiet, serenity, and calm.

Transformation - A marked change in nature, condition, or function.

Triumph - A great victory or achievement; success.

Trust - Reliance on or confidence in the character or abilities of someone.

Truth - Conformity to fact or actuality; accuracy and honesty.

Understanding - Sympathetic recognition or comprehension of a fact or situation.

Unification - The process of being united or made into a whole.

Uplift - Elevate to a higher level or condition morally or spiritually.

Valor - Great courage when facing risks or adversity.

Victory - Achievement of mastery in a struggle or conflict.

Vigor - Healthy physical or mental energy; vitality.

Virtue - Behavior showing high moral standards and goodness.

Vision - The ability to think optimistically about the future.

Vitality - Exuberant physical strength and mental vigor.

Well-Being - A state of health, happiness, and prosperity.

Willpower - The strength of will to carry out one's decisions or goals.

Wisdom - Knowledge and experiential understanding combined with insight.

Wonder - A feeling of amazement and admiration.

Zeal - Great energy and enthusiasm in pursuit of a goal.